LINCOLN CHRISTIAN COLLEGE AND SEMINARY

A Little Child
Shall Lead Them

P9-DDI-207

A Little Child Shall Lead Them

Hopeful Parenting in a Confused World

Johann Christoph Arnold

IVP

InterVarsity Press
Downers Grove, Illinois

Plough Publishing House
Farmington, Pennsylvania

© 1997 BY THE PLOUGH PUBLISHING HOUSE
OF THE BRUDERHOF FOUNDATION
FARMINGTON PA 15437, USA
ROBERTSBRIDGE, EAST SUSSEX TN32 5DR U.K.

PUBLISHED JOINTLY IN NORTH AMERICA
BY THE PLOUGH PUBLISHING HOUSE
AND INTERVARSITY PRESS,
P.O. BOX 1400, DOWNERS GROVE, IL 60515

ALL RIGHTS RESERVED

No part of this book may be reproduced in any form
without written permission from The Plough Publishing House.

InterVarsity Press® is the book-publishing division of InterVarsity Christian
Fellowship®, a student movement active on campus at hundreds of universities,
colleges and schools of nursing in the United States of America, and a member
movement of the International Fellowship of Evangelical Students. For information
about local and regional activities, write Public Relations Dept., InterVarsity
Christian Fellowship, 6400 Schroeder Rd., P.O. Box 7895, Madison, WI 53707-7895

Cover Photograph: David DeLossy/Image Bank

InterVarsity Press: ISBN 0-8308-1906-1
The Plough Publishing House: ISBN 0-87486-078-4
Printed in the United States of America

Library of Congress Cataloging-in-Publication Data
Arnold, Johann Christoph. 1940–
    A little child shall lead them: hopeful parenting in a confused world/
    by Johann Christoph Arnold
    p. cm.
    Includes bibliograhical references (p.).
    ISBN 0-87486-078-4 (pbk.)
    1.Christian education of children. 2. Parenting–Religious aspects–Christianity.
3. Family–Religious aspects–Christianity. 4.Bruderhof Communities–Education.
I. Title.
BV1475.2.A77 1996
248.8'45–DC20   96-23805
                                                              CIP

15 14 13 12 11 10 9 8 7 6 5 4 3 2 1
06 05 04 03 02 01 00 99 98 97

To my parents,
whose reverence for the childlike spirit
and love for children
has provided a rock for many
to stand on.

97249

Table of Contents

Introduction

EVERYWHERE IN SOCIETY TODAY we can see the fruits of an unguided and unloved generation. The problems need hardly be named: they are the daily fare of every newspaper and, increasingly, they affect the homes of even the most protected, privileged children. Solutions to the crisis (for it is really nothing less) are abundant. Bookstore shelves groan with new volumes on parenting, family therapists are in high demand, and politicians of every party compete to defend our families and to lament the loss of "traditional values."

Yet something is drastically wrong. Somewhere along the line we have forgotten what childhood is all about. In our preoccupation with adult solutions, we have lost sight of our children – of their vulnerability and innocence, their joyousness, and their love. We have lost touch with the childlike spirit.

Despite the words we use to describe the process of education – words like "parenting," "child rearing," and other such terms – it seems that in real life we grown-ups often learn as much from our children as they learn from us. In a certain sense, this is how it should be. Anyone who has raised children knows that education is a two-way street. By bursting the balloons of our theories, they constantly bring us back down to earth when we have become idealistic; and in constantly prodding us for answers to everything from "why is it bedtime?" to "what happens when you die?" they give us plenty of questions to think about ourselves.

Questions are what started this book. It is the result of hundreds of letters I have received over the years asking for advice about children and child rearing, and the input of dozens of parents, grandparents, and teachers. It is also the result of wisdom gained from living among children.

At the Bruderhof,* the Christian community movement to which I belong, several hundred families and single adults live, work, and eat together, sharing all things in common in the manner of the early church. Over half of our number (approx. 2500) is made up of children and young adults. As an elder and counselor – and as a father of eight and grandfather of fourteen – I keep in close touch with our nurseries, our kindergartens, and our schools on a daily basis. Unusual as this may seem, it is commonplace in our community.

Children are an important part of the reason we live together. In fact, it could even be said that in a practical sense they are the center of our life together. Certainly this does not mean that we raise them to think they are the center of the universe. Like children anywhere, they quarrel and fight, sulk and tease, and they are often in need of a firm hand. Yet it does mean that wherever we can, we strive to find their hearts, to turn potential conflicts into opportunities for nurture, and to remember that we are as dependent on God and his guidance as they are on ours. It also means recognizing that more often than not it is our children who lead us and point us toward the real answers: to openness,

*See appendix "About the Bruderhof," p. 181.

generosity, and unconditional trust. Time and again, it is they who help us to rediscover the simple truths that we adults so easily lost along the way. My grandfather Eberhard Arnold writes:

> It is children who lead us to the gospel...We are not worthy to educate them. Our lips are unclean; our dedication is not wholehearted. Our truthfulness is partial; our love divided. Our kindness is not without motives. We ourselves are not yet free of lovelessness, possessiveness, and selfishness...Only wise men and saints, only those who stand as children before God, are really fit to live and work with children.[1]

In a world that has grown increasingly cold and unchildlike, it is no easy thing to raise even one child, to guide him or her through the early years and the turmoil of adolescence. Yet whenever we open our hearts to the little ones around us, and whenever we stop to listen to them, we will discover that the challenges and trials they bring with them are always outweighed by greater joys and blessings. Inasmuch as we allow them to guide us with their simplicity, humility, and love, we will find that they can give us new hope and new courage.

J. Christoph Arnold
Rifton, New York

CHAPTER ONE

The Childlike Spirit

Then children were brought to him so that he could lay his hands on them and pray. The disciples rebuked the people, but Jesus said, "Let the children come to me, and do not hinder them; for the kingdom of heaven belongs to them" (Mt. 19:13–14).

IT IS HARD TO THINK of a more wonderful insight into the significance of children than these words of Jesus. Not only do they show his great love for every individual child, but also the importance of all children as the heirs to God's future. Yet what promise do they hold for us who are not children? Jesus' words become clearer to us when we understand what he means by "children": he is not speaking merely of immature human beings, but of every person who is willing to recognize that he or she is a child of God.

Once we have accepted the fact that we are children of God, our relationship to him will be like that of small children to their father and mother. Like children, we will open doors and enter them; like children, we will ask for what we need, and accept whatever is given to us; like children, we will not doubt the motives of others, but trust them.

In Matthew 7:7–11, Jesus says:

> Ask, and it will be given you; seek and you will find; knock, and it will be opened to you. For everyone who asks receives, and he who seeks finds, and to him who knocks it will be opened. Or what man of you, if his child asks him for bread, will give him a stone? Or if he asks for a fish, will give him a serpent? If you then, who are evil, know how to give good gifts to your children, how much more will your Father who is in heaven give good things to those who ask him!

Though not speaking directly about children, this passage can help us to understand what it means to be a true child.

In Matthew 18 we see that although the disciples wanted to learn from Jesus, they were not ready to become like children: they quarreled about who was the greatest among them, and who would be the greatest in the kingdom of God. In answer, Jesus called a little child and set him in their midst, and said to them, "Whoever humbles himself like this child is the greatest in the kingdom of heaven" (Mt. 18:4).

It is easy to look at the disciples and distance oneself from their unchildlike behavior – to think, "I've never wanted to be at the top." But if we are honest we must admit that each of us has been tempted by the same thoughts, by the same desire to be looked up to, to be important, to have power. And unless we cleanse our hearts of these desires, we cannot enter the kingdom of God. Unless we are ready to go the lowly way of Jesus, who came down to earth in the form of a helpless baby and died a death of public humiliation on a cross, we will not be let in.

The way of Jesus demands honesty and humility. Children possess both. They are as transparent as an open book; they stand in front of you with wide-open eyes and let you look freely into their souls. Most children say immediately what they feel. They will not say one thing to your face and another behind your back. Their childlikeness simply will not permit them to do otherwise.

Jesus also calls for a forgiving heart. He speaks of forgiving our brother seventy times seven. Here again it is children, and childlike people, who are often far ahead of the rest of us. As the German pastor Blumhardt* once pointed out, we grownups tend to latch on to every little upsetting thing and to brood over it.[2] Children may have a temper tantrum now and then, but once they get over it, it is as if nothing had ever happened. Any adult who has ever asked a child's forgiveness will have experienced how readily and unconditionally a child can forgive. In letting the forgiving spirit of a child overwhelm us, we become aware of our own corrupted nature and understand why we should become like children: God wants us to regain the childlike spirit – never to lose courage, and always to dare a new beginning.

Perhaps one of the most important things we can learn from children, especially in our modern world, where selfish

*Christoph Friedrich Blumhardt (1842–1919), Lutheran pastor, author, and influential Religious Socialist.

3

individualism is the order of the day, is their simple, unself-conscious way of responding to every situation from the heart. Naturalist Loren Eiseley illustrates this simplicity in his story of a Mediterranean villager who walked along the beach every morning, lifting stranded starfish from the sand and throwing them, one by one, back to the safety of the surf: "Saved that one. Saved that one..." Here was a grown man with the heart of a child.[3]

Jonathan Kozol says, "Someone, I don't know who, once said, 'If you seek God, look for a child.' Children...have a spiritual cleanness about them that makes them seem like messengers from somewhere else."[4] We adults often fail to grasp how near children are to God. We forget that, as Jesus says, "their angels always have access to my Father." "Angel" means "messenger." Guardian angels are spiritual messengers, spirits sent by God to protect and guide children. Unlike these angels, and unlike children, who see into the heart of God through their angels, we cannot see God. Yet we can see children, and we can receive them into our hearts. And in receiving them, we will receive Jesus himself (Lk. 9:48).

Anyone who raises children, educates them, or spends time with them can observe their capacity for love, trust, honesty, and forgiveness, and find joy in them. But all too often we forget Jesus' words about learning from them: "Unless you become like a child, you will not enter the kingdom of heaven" (Mt. 18:3). For the sake of children everywhere, one wishes that the kingdom might come very soon, so that all of them could go right in.

CHAPTER TWO

Founding a Family

FOR CENTURIES, people of all races and creeds have held that the health of a society – its social, cultural, and economic institutions, and its very moral fiber – is dependent on the health of its families. In recent years, however, increasing numbers of people have come to view the family, in particular the heterosexual marriage, as outdated and even oppressive. In fact, as author Maggie Gallagher points out, the family is being "ruthlessly dismantled, piece by piece," by those who believe that the abolition of marriage is "necessary to advance human freedom."[5]

Thankfully there are still plenty of people who realize that the traditional definition of the family is not only workable, but vital, and that in any case the answer to our problems does not lie in redefining it, but in returning to the simple teachings of Christ, who said, "Love God," and "Love your neighbor as yourself."

Yet the question of the two-parent family is a painful one for many. According to current statistics, about half of the married readers of this book will have experienced (or will one day experience) divorce. All the more, it is necessary to witness to the possibility of lasting, loving marriages – not in a judgmental way, but in the sense of taking a new look at God's will for each of us. Even if our generation has suffered tremendous anguish over our parents' marriages and our own, we must have hope and faith that wounds can be healed, sins forgiven, and God's plan for marriage reclaimed – for the sake of ourselves and our children, and for the sake of the whole world.

In his "Wedding Sermon from Prison," Bonhoeffer says:

> Marriage is more than your love for each other. It has a higher dignity and power, for it is God's holy ordinance… In your love you see only your two selves in the world, but in marriage you are a link in the chain of the generations which God causes to come and to pass away to his glory, and calls into his kingdom. In your love you see only the heaven of your own happiness, but in marriage you are placed at a post of responsibility toward the world and mankind…Marriage is more than something personal…
>
> Welcome one another, as Christ has welcomed you, for the glory of God…In a word, live together in the forgiveness of your sins, for without it no human fellowship, least of all a marriage, can survive. Don't insist on your rights, don't blame each other, don't judge or condemn each other, don't find fault with each other, but accept each other as you are, and forgive each other every day from the bottom of your hearts.[6]

When a couple founds a family on this basis, marriage (and parenthood) will be a joy, and light and strength will go out from their home into many others.

For a marriage to endure, God must lead the man and woman to each other, and they must want him to hold them together. They must also desire his order in their marriage, the husband serving his wife as spiritual head of the family, and his wife serving him in return as his helpmate. Such a relationship is possible only if Christ himself leads them both.

If a husband is to lead his wife aright, which means leading her to God, he must respect and love her, not rule over her in a domineering or assertive way. He must allow himself to be guided by the Holy Spirit and remember that true leadership means service. The apostle Peter warns us that unless we consider and honor our wives, our prayers may be hindered (1 Pet. 3:7). Likewise, a woman should love and respect her husband.

Prayer is crucial in keeping a marriage healthy. Husband and wife should pray together daily – for their children, for each other, and for those around them. Given the hectic pace of so many marriages today, it may be helpful to set aside regular times for prayer: every morning before breakfast, for instance, and every night before going to sleep. Of course, one can pray at other times during the day, too, wherever one happens to be. Being busy, or tired, is not an excuse when it comes to prayer. How many of us spend time reading the paper every evening but have no time for our spouse or for God?

Because of the emotional ups and downs that affect even the most stable relationship at times, both partners must continually seek Christ. His love reaches far beyond the bounds of fickle human love. Naturally we cannot only seek him; we must really obey him: "Every one who hears these words of mine *and does them* will be like a wise man who has built his house upon the rock" (Mt. 7:24). When things are going well, obedience is easy. But what about hard times? Every person, every parent, has a cross to carry in life: sickness, loss of a spouse or child; the inability to have children; a broken relationship with one's partner, parents, relatives, or friends. But if, like Simon of Cyrene (Lk. 23:26), we are willing to accept our cross and carry it for the sake of Christ, he will give us the courage we need to come through every difficult situation.

Many people pray for God's will, but follow it only when it fits with their own will. If we really love God, we will seek to follow him no matter what the outcome; we will sense that our deepest joy and greatest security lies in being faithful to him at all costs. In turning to God, we will always find new forgiveness, new humility, and new strength to set our marriages straight when they begin to falter. He is the only sure foundation on which to build a family and raise children.[7]

CHAPTER THREE

The Unborn Child

THE NINE MONTHS OF WAITING for a baby can deepen a couple's relationship and bring them closer to each other than any other time in their marriage. After all, the development of a baby in its mother's womb is far more than a biological process, even though that in itself is almost too great to comprehend. Especially for a young couple looking forward to their first child, there is a sense of excitement, the thrill of the unknown, a strange mixture of anxiety and expectant joy. There is also awe before the mystery of new life and the responsibility of parenthood.

In Psalm 139:13–16 we read:

You created my inmost being; you knit me together in my mother's womb. I praise you because I am fearfully and wonderfully made; your works are wonderful, I know that full well. My frame was not hidden from you when I was made in the secret place. When I was woven together in the depths of the earth, your eyes saw my unformed body.

All the days ordained for me were written in your book before one of them came to be.

In his book *Inner Land,* my grandfather Eberhard Arnold describes the unborn child not merely as a developing fetus, but as a little soul – a being for whom we must have reverence.

For the unborn as much as for the living child, a secure, loving family life is of great importance. Even while still in the womb, an unborn child can suffer if he or she does not feel nurturing love and tenderness. Psychologists and educators have long warned of the negative effects of broken homes on children, and more and more of them recognize that the effects may be no less serious for the unborn.

According to the Gospel of Luke, an unborn child can share in the emotions of its mother:

> When Elizabeth heard Mary's greeting, the child leaped in her womb. And Elizabeth was filled with the Holy Spirit and exclaimed with a loud cry, "Blessed are you among women, and blessed is the fruit of your womb. And why has this happened to me, that the mother of my Lord comes to me? For as soon as I heard the sound of your greeting, the child in my womb leaped for joy" (Lk. 1:41–44).

In a similar vein, German author Joseph Lucas writes that a mother's thoughts are passed on to her child while it is still in the womb. Everything good in her – her love, her purity, her strength – are planted into the child's being before it is born. In a certain way, he writes, a mother's life during pregnancy lays the foundation for all later education. What comes after birth is "the unfurling and developing of what has already germinated in the soul."[8]

In all children, but especially in the unborn child, we can sense the reality of the link between human life and eternity. In awaiting the birth of a baby, we await, as the Indian poet Tagore says, the renewed message that God has not yet lost faith in humankind.

CHAPTER FOUR

Birth

EVERY TIME A BABY IS BORN, eternity comes down to our world. We feel joy in the miracle of a new human being and know that, in receiving an innocent soul, we have received something from the hand of the Creator himself – a life of unknown length in which, as poet Philip Britts writes, "a new note will be sounded, a new color revealed."[9]

No matter how difficult the circumstances of a birth, a baby's trusting gaze reminds us of God's love and tenderness. It is as if he or she is surrounded by the pure air of heaven. We can only marvel at the mystery of birth, at the fact that a new life has been given which has in it something unique and original from God.

Sometimes our modern, technologically-oriented way of looking at things reduces their meaning. For example, many people see birth as a merely biological process set into motion by sexual union. Isn't there more to it? We are reminded of God's role in the mystery of new life every time a childless couple – after years of trying to bear children with the help of medical science – leave their longing in God's hand and then experience the untold joy of receiving a child.

Dorothy Day writes that "even the most hardened, the most irreverent, is awed by the stupendous fact of creation. No matter how cynically or casually the worldly may treat the birth of a child, it remains spiritually and physically a tremendous event."[10]

In our Bruderhof communities, newborn infants are brought to a special church service where their fathers and mothers present them to the congregation. In being "given" to the church, the children are given into its care and keeping. The church then returns each one to his or her parents to be raised by them in the love of God. To us, the act is more than symbolic. Ultimately, our children do not belong to us. They are gifts entrusted to us by God.

CHAPTER FIVE

Motherhood

A TRUE MOTHER thinks day and night about the well-being of her children. She is the first to praise them and to comfort them, and also the first to protect them when she senses that they may be in danger. It is she who has carried them and borne the pains of pregnancy and child-birth, and it is she who now continues to carry them in her heart. Her intuition is often clearer than her husband's, and she will not let him make light of her concerns or reassure her too easily. She will also be the first to turn to God on a child's behalf. Perhaps that is what inspired the old Jewish saying, "God could not be everywhere at once, so he gave each child a mother."

When a child cries at night, it is usually the mother who will be at his or her bedside first. She feels her child's pain, instinctively, and she will bear it not only as a burden, but also as a privilege and a joy.

A mother's sensitivity and love is boundless. She will continue to keep her children on her heart long after others have given up on them. Like St. Augustine's mother Monica, who refused to disown him during his years of youthful rebellion, she will continue to have hope for a prodigal son (or daughter) even when everyone else has condemned him. Moreover, she will believe for him when he has ceased to believe.

I cannot thank God enough for the love of my mother, and for her deep relationship with my father. Even though they were sparing in their use of religious language (they never talked about their piety), it was obvious to us seven children that they loved God, one another, and each of us. And while it was clear that our father was head of the family, he never tolerated the slightest disrespect from us towards our mother.

Mumia Abu-Jamal, a contemporary African-American writer who grasps the importance of the mother and the family as few people do, says that a mother's love "is the foundation of every love: it is the primary relationship of all human love, the first love we experience and, as such, a profound influence on all subsequent and secondary relationships in life." It is, he says, an unconditional love "that surpasses all reason."[11]

Many women in our time rebel against motherhood. They forget that it is not only a God-given task, but a God-given privilege as well. Motherhood was once regarded as the noblest calling of a woman; nowadays, it is pushed aside by more "desirable" careers and seen as an inconvenience or even an embarrassment. It is true that many women rebel because of the oppression and lovelessness of the men around them, but in the end their resentment, understandable as it may be, achieves little. How different family life could be if we admitted to our confusion about the role of man and of woman; if we sought to rediscover *God's* plan for both, and regarded one another with respect and love!

In our communities, mothers participate in the daily work as fully as possible – as cooks and nurses, doctors and seamstresses, accountants, teachers, graphic designers, and secretaries. Yet when pregnancy requires it, their first priority is always motherhood. Far from regretting or resenting it, they feel, as all of us do, that it is a gift; that in God's eyes, there is no sacrifice more worthy than that made for the sake of a child.

Fatherhood

UNBELIEVABLE AS IT MAY SEEM, half of our nation's children will spend at least part of their childhood without a father in the home. Never before in our history have so many men abandoned the children they fathered. Fathers are vanishing from their children's lives, not just physically, but legally as well. The number of paternity suits is steadily on the rise, and the problem of "deadbeat dads" is taking on the proportions of a national catastrophe.

Not surprisingly, many of the same people who complain about the loss of "family values" have abandoned wives and children themselves, often through divorce and remarriage. Despite their words, their actions send the message that fatherhood is simply not a priority to them. In some cases, even their words betray them. Instead of speaking about "deadbeat dads," they speak about "illegitimate children" and "unwed mothers" – terms that conveniently shift the burden of stigma and guilt away from themselves and onto the woman and child. Is anyone ever "illegitimate" in God's eyes?

As a nation, we have lost something precious. In previous centuries, fathers were seen as irreplaceable. They may not have been primary caregivers, but they bore the ultimate responsibility for the well-being of their wives and children. In the last one hundred years this has changed fundamentally. In a century marked by war, political unrest, and unprecedented opportunities for travel, more children than ever before have grown up without a father in the house.

True fatherhood, of course, entails far more than being physically present in the life of a child. There are plenty of men who, because they do not relate to their children, are emotionally absent, even though they may live in the same house with them. How many fathers are there today who confuse their children's hunger for love and attention with the desire for material things? All too often, in an attempt to make up for long absences or to still a guilty conscience, men send home gifts, when what their children really long for is a hug, a smile, or a story at bedtime.

One of the things children need most in a father is someone who can see the world through a child's eyes. Author Ralph Kinney Bennett writes:

> This is one of the most overlooked rules for a father. Go back to your childhood, and you begin to understand why so many things are mysterious, frightening, or even funny to a child...
>
> Fathers who forget the child's point of view are nonplused, for instance, when they buy their daughter an

expensive toy, only to see her spend hours playing with the box the toy came in – except that it isn't a box; it's a castle. Fathers would do well to remember when their wagon was really a stagecoach, or their bed a spaceship.[12]

In the first five years of my life, my father's work kept him away from home for a total of three years. Although I know this had certain negative effects on my early childhood, I have never doubted my father's love. We were separated physically, but he remained a positive presence in my life.

Any true relationship between a father and his child is deeply dependent on the father's relationship to God. It is God who made him a father, and he must feel an inner assurance that it is his duty to be the head of his family. A father who lacks moral character or is unsure of himself cannot provide his children with real security. This is not to say he should be authoritarian. Even when he needs to hold his ground on an issue – even when he is setting necessary boundaries and limits – he must always be sensitive and have a heart for his children.

Fatherhood begins before the birth of a child. During his wife's pregnancy, which is often a period of anxiety and uncertainty, a husband should do his utmost to show her his love in practical ways around the house, especially when she feels nauseated, fatigued, or emotionally distraught. If she carries the added burden of medical complications and needs bed rest, he should be ready to take on still more. Needless to say, he should carry his wife's pregnancy in an inner way by giving encouragement and reassurance. And he should pray daily both for his wife and for the baby.

Once the baby arrives, his main task is to provide for his family with loving strength and security. He should not forget that Jesus, the only true man, was not afraid to apply to himself the image of a hen gathering her chicks, and he should live at all times in a manner worthy of him.

Author Michael Phillips asks, "How long does God expect us to father our children? Until they are financially independent? Until they leave home? Until they get in trouble?...Once we become fathers, we remain fathers until the day we die."[13] Let us recognize that fatherhood is a life-long responsibility, and remember who gave it to us.

CHAPTER SEVEN

Creating a Home

IT IS ONE THING to have children. To create a true home, a place of love and security, is quite a different matter. Unfortunately, many adults lack a sense of what this means. They have no time for their children and, if they are married, not even for their spouse. They are always "too busy." Some parents are so preoccupied with their jobs that even when they do see their children at the end of a long day, they have no energy to be available for them. They may sit in the same room with their children, but their minds are still back at their place of work, and one eye is on the evening news.

Parents who love their children will be determined to be with them as regularly as possible – and to be there *for* them. Indoor activities like reading aloud, working on hobbies, and above all eating together give vital opportunities for interaction and a sense of togetherness. So do outdoor activities like basketball, tennis, fishing, or backpacking. They provide the sort of positive experiences that children will not forget as they grow up, marry, and raise their own families.

Birthdays, graduations, and other similar occasions are a very important part of home life, too. Aside from simply being happy times, they are events that nurture and help children grow; times when we can thank God for them and let them know how much we love and appreciate them and celebrate their lives. In general, however, it is the priorities we set in our everyday lives that have the greatest impact on our children. A woman recently wrote to me:

> My father, like most men of his generation, chose to immerse himself in his career: he was a naval officer. I can remember very vividly the times that he really took time to be with us. Because they were so few, each one was very special. We loved our father very much; he was so attentive and gentle when he was at home. At the time we didn't feel ignored; it seemed quite normal that he had to work every weekend or be away for a month to a year at a time. Now that I'm an adult I wonder what he sacrificed all that time for. A career? His country? Certainly not for the money. It strikes me as selfishness masked as duty. Yet I am sure that if my marriage had continued and we would have had children, my husband and I would have done the very same thing. It's considered "normal" in middle- and upper middle-class families to put one's career first.

Sometimes, creating a space for "family time" with your children will require putting your foot down, especially when they are playing outdoors with their friends, for instance, and you call them in for dinner. Once a routine has been established, though, children will look forward to it. Among my best childhood memories are the evenings our family would sit outside and listen to our father tell us stories about Jesus, about the early Christian martyrs, and about other men and women through the ages who suffered for their faith. We lived in the backwoods of Paraguay, in South America, and there was no electricity. When darkness came, abrupt and early as it does in the subtropics, we lit candles and continued to sit in the flickering light. Our house was not far from the edge of a forest, and often we heard wild animals in the distance. When we were frightened we sang together, and our parents told us of the courage that comes from having a personal relationship with God – something that became a reality for us.

No matter how a family chooses to spend its time together, a few minutes at bedtime are always crucial. Younger children need the security of a good-night kiss, a reassuring word, and a short prayer before they go to sleep. Children who are afraid of the dark or of being alone, especially those who are not able or willing to express their fears, should be reminded that they have guardian angels watching over them.

True security, though, depends on more than comforting words. Children find the deepest emotional and inner security when their parents' love is demonstrated in deeds – not just at bedtime, but from day to day. Speaking of family life in general, Mother Teresa says:

> We must not think that our love has to be extraordinary. But we do need to love without getting tired. How does a

lamp burn? Through the continuous input of small drops of oil. These drops are the small things of daily life: faithfulness, small words of kindness, a thought for others, our way of being quiet, of looking, of speaking, and of acting. They are the true drops of love that keep our lives and relationships burning like a lively flame.[14]

CHAPTER EIGHT

The Role of Grandparents

AFTER THE MOTHER, the most wonderful thing God created is the grandmother – at least many children think so. Everyone loves grandparents. It is over their roles that people begin to disagree. Many families are blinded by the common misconception that in-laws cannot get along together, and in accepting this stereotype as fact, they hurt what could otherwise be a meaningful relationship. Doesn't God want us all to live side by side in peace? After all, he meant husband and wife to be one, and naturally each of them has parents.

At the Bruderhof, where hundreds of children grow up with grandparents on both sides, we have found that the extended family can be a tremendous blessing. In my own family, for instance, six of our eight children are married and starting their own families. My wife and I have great joy in our fourteen grandchildren. Yet it is clear to us that no matter how much we love them, we must let our children find their own way in bringing them up.

To other grandparents, let me say this: don't forget that raising your grandchildren is your children's responsibility first and foremost – not yours – and that their ideas may be different from yours. At the same time, though, young couples should be encouraged to turn to their parents for advice. Why shouldn't grandparents, who have raised children themselves, pass on their wisdom, even if much of it was gained through mistakes?

Though grandparents should feel free to advise, they should never interfere. (Obviously there are exceptions; for example, situations in which an irresponsible or abusive parent has left a grandparent with no choice but to intervene.) Often the best help is an offer to support in practical ways: when a grandchild is sick, for instance, or when the parents have been taxed to their limits for whatever reason. Every grandchild delights in some special attention – a story, a cookie, extra help with homework, or a walk outdoors. Grandparents who live far away from their grandchildren will need to find other ways to show love – an occasional post card or gift, or perhaps weekly or monthly phone calls. Regardless of a child's age, time spent with a grandfather or grandmother is always enriching. For the child, it provides an oasis of comfort and quiet, and for the grandparents, an opportunity to love and to be loved in return. It is a blessing for both.

CHAPTER NINE

The First Years

E DUCATORS HAVE LONG HELD that the first years of a
child's life are by far the most formative; that whatever
a child experiences in this period will influence the rest of
his or her life in fundamental ways. The nineteenth-century
German educational reformer Froebel even writes that
a person's spiritual life is formed to a great degree by the experiences of early childhood: whether he or she turns out to
be gentle or violent, industrious or lazy, dull or creative, per-
sonable or antisocial. The child's future relations to father
and mother, to other family members, to society and
humankind, to nature, and to God depend chiefly on his or
her development in this period.[15]

Not surprisingly, recent studies have confirmed this sci-
entifically. In light of this fact and the tremendous
responsibility it places on every parent, it is vital that the
bonds between father, mother, and baby are nurtured from
the first days of infancy. Parents should remember that God

has given the child to *them,* and that it is primarily their responsibility to guide the child toward choosing a path that fulfills God's purpose for him or her.

The significance of interacting with a baby cannot be emphasized enough. My mother always said that education starts in the cradle. Babies should be held, stroked, and caressed. They should be sung to, talked to, and smiled at. Most important, they should be loved unconditionally. (Many readers will remember a well-known research project done with monkeys in the 1960s: those that were cuddled and stroked even by robots gained weight faster and developed more sturdily than those who were socially isolated and fed through the bars. If this is true for monkeys, how much truer for people!)

As children become toddlers, they should be stimulated and encouraged with simple games, rhymes, and songs. Because a child's mental potential at this stage is unrivaled by later stages, whatever he or she does not absorb now will be absorbed only with greater difficulty later. That is why the experts speak of a "window of opportunity" that will never be opened as widely again. To be sure, development cannot be measured only in terms of learning or achievement. A child's emotional and spiritual development is equally important.

Just as much as small children need stimulation and guidance, they need time to be by themselves. Hours spent in daydreams and quiet play instill in a child a sense of security and provide a necessary lull in the rhythm of the day. All too often, grown-ups needlessly disturb and pester children with their intrusions. Some people cannot seem to pass a baby without picking it up, holding, kissing, or doing something to it. When he or she resists or struggles, they feel hurt, and what was a happy scene moments before becomes one of frustration.

At every point of contact, loving consideration for the inner disposition of the child – for the childlike spirit of simplicity, honesty, and vulnerability – is the crucial element. Raising children should never mean trying to mold them according to our own wishes and ideas. It should mean helping them to become what they already are in God's mind. Jane Clement, a poet and teacher in the Bruderhof schools for many years, expresses this thought beautifully in one of her poems:

Child, though I take your hand
and walk in the snow;
though we follow the track of the mouse together,
though we try to unlock together the mystery
of the printed word, and slowly discover
why two and three makes five
always, in an uncertain world –

child, though I am meant to teach you much,

what is it, in the end,
except that together we are
meant to be children
of the same Father

and I must unlearn
all the adult structure
and the cumbering years

and you must teach me
to look at the earth and the heaven
with your fresh wonder.[16]

"Unlearning" our adult mindsets is never easy. Even the disciples were indignant when children pushed through them to get close to Jesus. When there are children around, things don't always go as planned. Furniture gets scratched, flower beds trampled, new clothes torn, toys lost or broken. Children want to handle things and play with them. They want to have fun; they need space to be rambunctious and noisy.

To parents of small children, the first years can seem overwhelmingly strenuous at times. At the end of a long day, children can even seem more of a bother than a gift. After all, they are not porcelain dolls, but rascals with sticky fingers and runny noses who sometimes cry at night. Yet if we have children, we must welcome them as they are.

BED-WETTING

Although bed-wetting is a natural phase of childhood and widespread not only among toddlers, but also among older children, many parents exhibit an unfortunate lack of understanding for it. According to one disturbing study, up to a third of parents deal with their children's bed-wetting by punishing them for it. In fact, cases of serious and even fatal child abuse have been attributed to bed-wetting or soiling incidents.[17]

Bed-wetting is more common in boys than in girls. The majority will have conquered it by the age of seven, and when this is the case, parents should be thankful. In many instances, however, it continues. Sometimes it may be the result of parental pressures such as perfectionism, overanxiety, or premature or improper attempts at toilet training. In rare cases, it can be the result of an infection of the bladder, or even a kidney disorder. Generally, though, it is simply a delayed maturation of the nervous system.

If bed-wetting persists in an older child and there are indications that the problem is a medical one, consult a family physician. Be aware, too, that even after a long period of dryness, emotional trauma such as the death of a close friend or relative, or divorce, or the birth of a new sibling (or even much less apparent events) can cause a recurrence. When this happens, the child will be especially discouraged, and it is vital that his parents help him with love and reassurance.

Because bed-wetting can be traumatic for an older child, especially when he is invited to spend the night with a friend or relative, parents must be sure to reassure the child that they are confident the problem will eventually be conquered and that it does not diminish him as a person.

A child should never be punished for bed wetting. In stead of helping to overcome the problem, punishment will only compound it by drawing undue attention to it and adding to the feelings of shame and insecurity already present. Finally, remember that there is no method that will help in every case: as a rule, overcoming bed-wetting simply takes time and patience on the part of both parents and child.

CHAPTER TEN

Teaching Respect

A LL OF US ARE FAMILIAR with the biblical commandment that is the cornerstone of child rearing: honor father and mother. But what does it mean? On one level, of course, it simply means that children must learn respect. To small children, father and mother stand for God; if they do not honor them, how can they ever learn to honor him? On another, it places a burden on every parent: the responsibility of seeing that this commandment is obeyed.

Honor starts with respect for authority, with the "fear of God" and the similar "fear" of parents, who raise them in God's stead. Obviously this is not to say that children should be afraid of God or their parents. It means that as they grow up they must overcome their inborn self-centeredness and learn to yield to others when the situation calls for it. They must find a willingness to submit that is born – even if they are unaware of it – of love and reverence.

If respect is achieved by authoritarian means, it will eventually breed anger and rebellion. Like any other virtue, it must be taught by example and fostered in an atmosphere of trust. It is something gained only with time and effort.

Yet because respect is a basic part of every wholesome relationship, it is vital that it be fostered from a very early age. In my experience, it must be established well within the first four years. In most families with young children the task will fall to the mother, since she is the one most likely to be at home with them during the working day. A husband should always do his part to support his wife's authority, but it is imperative that she establish it in her own right as well, and insist on respect and obedience from her children in every instance.

At times this can be easily done, simply by appealing to (or affirming) the natural love of the child, or by guiding him or her with a gentle word. Just as frequently, however, it will demand a struggle. The most important thing, then, is that the struggle is fought and won. Disrespect may seem manageable in small children (you can always send them to their room until they are willing to listen to you) but in a rebellious teenager it may only be overcome with a painful contest of wills. If a battle seems inevitable, it should not be avoided, but fought through.

Just a word of caution, though. Remember that respect must be earned, and that when children lack respect for adults, it is usually because the adults in their lives lack respect for them. Clyde Haberman, a reporter who has talked extensively with children and teens in New York City, says it is hardly surprising that so many students these days have little or no respect for teachers: in many cases, their own parents inspire very little respect or love [18]

Even if you feel you deserve a child's respect, never dig in your heels solely for the sake of asserting yourself. Your long-term relationship with the child is too important for that. In the end, you will achieve nothing unless your authority is grounded in love. My father J. Heinrich Arnold writes:

> If we as parents love God with all our heart and soul, our children will have the right reverence for us, and we will also have reverence for our children and for the wonderful mystery of becoming and being a child. Reverence for the spirit that moves between parent and child is the basic element of a true family life. [19]

CHAPTER ELEVEN

Spoiling Your Child

ESPITE THE FACT that millions of children around the globe grow up in acute poverty, most children in our western society still have far more than they need. We are raising a whole generation of what can only be called spoiled children. Parents are often quick to blame our materialistic society at large, or the steady diet of commercials their children see daily, but in actual fact the problems begin long before their children are exposed to these.

In my experience, pampered children are always the product of pampered parents – parents who insist on always getting their own way, and whose lives are structured around the illusion that instant gratification brings happiness. (Isn't that what going to the mall is all about?)

Children are spoiled not only by an overabundance of food, toys, clothing, and other material things. Many parents spoil their children simply by giving in to their whims.

When they are still in the playpen, this is bad enough, but as they grow older, the problem gets much worse. Children who feel relatively sure that they will get their way are bound to put up a good fight, and soon their wishes and demands define their entire relationship with their parents. How many harried parents spend all of their energy simply trying to keep up with their children's demands? And how many more give in to their children just to keep them quiet?

Other parents pamper their children by giving them too many choices. A child should be taught to make decisions – there is nothing wrong with that in itself – but to constantly offer him or her an array of choices is a disservice. Children who face several different brands of breakfast cereals or soft drinks every time they sit down to eat will not necessarily be any happier than those whose food is set before them. In fact, they are likely to be more finicky and unappreciative. Even if they are not aware of it, children crave limits: When their boundaries are clearly defined, they thrive.

It is also easy to spoil children by overstimulating them. Though children should be exposed to a variety of activities wide enough to keep their attention and to encourage their imagination, interest, and inquisitiveness, they should not be brought up in an unreal world. They must learn that in real life there are many things they simply cannot do or have.

Children who are given too much rein become little tyrants at home and at school, and as they grow older, they will go to any length to get what they want. All too soon, they will be impulsive, demanding teenagers, and what was once plain discontent turns into rebellion against all parental authority.

What is the best way to bring up children without pampering them? From the Book of Proverbs to the journals of modern medicine, the wisdom is the same: discipline your child. The results are obvious. Whereas spoiled children tend to be insecure, selfish, and dishonest, well-disciplined children are usually appreciative, considerate, and self-assured. Hebrews 12:6 says that God disciplines and chastises those whom he loves. If we really desire to love our children as God loves us, we will do the same.

CHAPTER TWELVE

Discipline

I N AN AGE WHEN DISCIPLINE of any kind is regarded by many as physical abuse, it is tempting to dismiss whole-sale the Old Testament proverbs about sparing the rod and spoiling the child. All the same, I believe that even if we re-ject physical punishment, we can find sound wisdom in the ones that speak about the importance of discipline in a gen-eral sense: "Reprove your child, for in this there is hope" (Prov. 19:18).

Whenever children are conscious of having done some-thing wrong and there are no consequences, they learn that they can get away with it. It is a terrible thing for a child to get that message. With younger ones, the issue might seem unimportant; their misdeed may actually be small, but the lessons they learn will have repercussions far into the future. An undisciplined six-year-old may only take cookies with-out asking, but at sixteen he or she may be shoplifting.

Discipline does not just mean catching children in the act and punishing them, however. Nor does it mean suppressing their will in favor of one's own or criticizing them continually and arguing with them when they talk back. It should not be viewed as a negative part of child rearing, but as a positive one. The goal of true discipline is to nurture a child's will for the good – to support and affirm him or her in choosing right over wrong. It means reinforcing the positive whenever possible by lending a helping hand.

Discipline must start early enough. Already in the first few months, babies find out that their crying summons attention and concern. A mother who lets herself be led to respond to every whimper has already lost the battle. (Obviously a baby needs to be soothed, but it need not be picked up every time it cries.) If children do not learn in the first years that their self-will must be controlled, when will they? To hold out firmly and consistently against a child's will is often irksome. It is always easier to let things slide. Yet parents who prize comfort above the effort of discipline will find that, in the long run, their children will become more and more troublesome.

How should a child be disciplined? How not? In my experience, one must avoid scolding a child frequently, especially for little things. Scolding often turns to nagging, which escalates to impatience and anger, and both parent and child will end up in a shouting match. Yelling at a child only encourages him to yell back.

One of the simplest forms of discipline is "time out" – putting a child who has misbehaved in another room or separating him or her in some way from others for a few minutes. Almost every time, the child will soon feel bored or lonely and want to return to his or her playmates or family. (Just don't forget about the child in the meantime.) And when the "time out" is over, don't dwell on it, but move on. Used consistently, "time out" can be one of the most effective tools of discipline for the toddler and preschool child: children this age tend to respond better to immediate action than to words. Certainly it can be used for older children as well, but it is probably not necessary or appropriate for a child under a year.

With regard to corporal punishment, let me make it clear that as far as I am concerned, beating a child is nothing less than physical abuse. Never spank a child unless he or she is your own, and never strike or even slap a child on the face or head. And if you do feel the need to spank on occasion, do it only as a last resort. A spank on the bottom (administered with one's hand) may be helpful for a small child now and then, especially when a parent is unable to stop unacceptable behavior by other means. Even such spanking is wrong, however, when administered in anger or impatience, or used frequently. Consider that your discipline will be productive only if the child feels your love as strongly as your desire to correct him or her. God sent the Hebrews not only the Law of Moses but also manna, the bread of heaven. Without such bread – that is, without

41

warmth and kindness, without respect, and without an appeal to the heart of a child – sooner or later any form of discipline will lead to rebellion.

Discipline achieves good results only when there is a relationship of trust between parent and child. Thankfully my siblings and I had such a relationship with our parents. Once, when I was around eight years old, I upset my father so much by something I did that he felt he needed to punish me severely. As he was about to spank me, I looked up at him and said, "Papa, I'm sorry. Do what you need to do. I know you still love me." To my astonishment, he leaned down and hugged me and said, "Son, I forgive you." My words had completely disarmed him. The incident taught me a lesson I have never forgotten, also in dealing with my own children: Don't be afraid to discipline your children, but the moment you feel remorse on their part, be sure there is forgiveness on yours.

Consistency is the key to effective discipline. Beware of giving mixed messages. If you disagree with your spouse over how to handle an incident, don't discuss it in front of your children – they will quickly learn to play you off against each other. Aside from creating confusion in a child's mind, inconsistency also prevents the formation of the boundaries that every young child needs. Even though he may resist at the beginning, he will thrive on routines once they are established.

Once you've said something, stick to it. When a child realizes that you don't really mean what you say, everything you do to try to control him or her will be useless, including your threats. Even when the living room is full of guests, don't be embarrassed if your child misbehaves. Frustrating as it may be, young children love to disobey just when their parents are hosting guests and planning a relaxed mealtime; bite your lip and do what you need to do. You will have to deal with your child anyway after the guests have gone, and your long-term relationship is far more important than the impression he or she makes on others.

Children need to learn early on that every action has consequences. This does not mean they can be expected to obey every command or request unquestioningly. When a child does not understand the reason for an admonition, it may be necessary to explain it to him or her. Sometimes, though, a child should have no choice but to obey. Then, if a direct conflict arises, it is imperative that you win. The main thing is that you as a parent set the limits and don't let your children set them for you. If you are able to enforce their limits consistently and with love, sooner or later they will be able to set them for themselves.

No matter how often you need to discipline your children, never humiliate them. Don't talk about their weaknesses or mistakes in front of other adults or their friends. Never compare them with other children, either to their face or in your own mind. It is easy to label a child as "difficult," but it is *never* right or just. Like children, we must not only forgive the wrongs of the previous hour and day, but also forget them. Like them, we must start every day anew.

CHAPTER THIRTEEN

Explaining Life, Death, and Suffering

IN SPEAKING ABOUT BIRTH, death, and other riddles of human existence with a young child, it is always good to remember that these mysteries lie in God's hands. Children are quicker than adults to understand this. Their minds are simple and unencumbered by adult ideas, and their questions can be answered simply and straightforwardly. The main thing is to assure them that all life comes from God and goes back to God, and that, because of this, they do not need to fear death. In my experience that is usually enough; to try to explain more or to speculate further may only confuse or worry them. Emphasize God's power over life and death, and point out the many passages in the Bible that tell us how wonderful it will be when Jesus comes back – how the trumpet will sound and we will all be made alive, more alive even than we are now. As they grow up and demand further explanation, especially about birth and human reproduction, answer their questions honestly, but don't burden them with more than they ask for.

At a surprisingly young age, children may ask questions like, "Why does God allow so much suffering in the world? Why does he allow poverty, war, and evil? Is God powerless? Is the devil stronger than God?" Although such thoughts may never even occur to some children, they will cause considerable worry to others.

When children ask about suffering, impress on them that, despite sickness and pain, poverty, war, and injustice, God is all-powerful, and that in the end his love will rule. Explain to them that all need and suffering in the world is a deep pain to God, especially the suffering of innocent people. Help them to see that it is not God's fault that people hate each other and start wars, for instance – it is our fault. Remind them of the story of Adam and Eve, who questioned God's command and then disobeyed him by eating from the tree of life after he had specifically forbidden them to do so. Tell them that this is how sin came into the world. Before the "fall" of man, everything and everyone lived in harmony and peace. That is how God wanted it to be, and that is how it will be again when his peaceable kingdom comes on the earth.

It never hurts to tell children, too, that even though we cannot understand suffering and death, we do know they are a part of God's plan. Naturally this should not be done in a way that might frighten them. All the same, it will not harm them to know that if they want to become fighters for

God's kingdom, they must be willing to make sacrifices for Christ's sake.

As children grow up, it is vital that they experience the faith of their parents. Without it, they will not have the assurance they need to cope with the suffering they are bound to face sooner or later. Every decade brings new tragedies and suffering – earthquakes and floods, hunger, wars, violence, and crime. Make time to talk with your child whenever you sense the slightest insecurity. Maybe his or her class has discussed a recent accident or natural disaster; maybe a classmate or relative has been injured or even died; maybe he or she has read or seen something frightening or traumatic. No matter how small the incident may seem to you, it may loom large in the child's mind. Listen to him or her, answer any questions he or she might have, and provide comfort and reassurance.

If you are able to bring the need of the world to your children in a way that helps them to understand the suffering of others, they will feel compassion rather than fear. And when they do express fear or worry, remind them that each of them has a guardian angel who has access to God on their behalf. Lastly, tell your children that God promised he will never burden us with more than we can bear. No matter how great a child's fears, he or she must be helped to believe that God is always there, and that our faith need never be shattered.

CHAPTER FOURTEEN

Religious Education

IN A WORLD that has grown increasingly pagan, many parents worry over their children's religious upbringing. To be sure, leading one's child to God is the most important task of every parent, but it is also the one in which it is the easiest to make grave mistakes. As the following sentences from Christoph Blumhardt show, the problem is often a matter of confusion: of people mistaking the religious traditions they have grown up with for the teachings of Jesus.

It is an illusion to think you are bringing a child to the Savior by rushing him to church and having him baptized. Millions of children are baptized but then grow up into the ways of their parents instead of in the ways of Jesus...You cannot bring your children to Christ if he lives only in your Bible or your private rituals and not in your heart. "Let the children come to me," says Jesus; not to your pious customs, your Christian traditions, but "to me."[20]

How, then, should parents lead a child to God? For one thing, never force religious instruction on your child. It is far more important for him to feel the impact of your own faith. God's Spirit does not let itself be tied down to the space of a lesson or text. As long as your faith is really living in you, you will not depend on pious words to pass it on to your children. They will sense it in your daily life and in your contact with them.

If a child is to develop a love for God, Jesus, and human-kind, he must be taught reverence for them. Often that can be done quite naturally by pointing them to nature. Jesus himself used parables and metaphors from nature to illustrate a point. Children will sense God behind a sunset or a starry sky; they will imagine angels in the roaring wind. They will be the first to perceive that behind the beauty of the earth is a creator, who dwells in their own hearts.

One can also bring God to children by reading them stories from the life of Jesus and by explaining to them the meaning of Christmas, Easter, and other celebrations with which they are already familiar. There is no better time than the weeks before Christmas, for instance, to read together the wonderful Old Testament prophecies of the coming Messiah (and to introduce them to Handel's *Messiah*), or to talk about the angel who appeared to Mary, the hosts that announced Christ's birth, and the guardian angel that each child has himself. In the same way that children relate to the story of Christmas, they can also understand something of the meaning of Easter: the suffering of Jesus, of Mary, and the disciples, and then the joy of the resurrection.

Along with reverence and love to God, teach your children gratefulness. Whether through grace at mealtimes or prayers at bedtime, urge them to thank God for all they have for parents and family, friends, a roof over their heads, clothes, food, and safety. Remind them, too, that not all children have what they have, and open their eyes to the needs of others. Assure them that God is their father and that he is accessible to each of us, whether old or young.

Finally, teach your children by reading to them from the Bible. As they grow older, encourage them to learn important passages by heart, and point out how this or that verse can provide a rock on which to stand later in life, especially during difficult times. Remember, though, that ultimately it is not memorized verses that will capture a child's heart, but the living example of adults who show love and respect for God and for each other in their deeds as well as their words. And never forget that often children are already much closer than we are to God.

CHAPTER FIFTEEN

When Children Suffer

There is something greater than raising the dead and feeding the multitudes: Blessed are they who have believed with their whole heart.
Fragment, "The Coptic Acts of Paul"[21]

ANYONE WHO HAS BEEN at the bedside of a mortally sick child will know what I mean when I write about the fight for life that goes on in each soul and body. This fight is independent of the parents' longing that the child live; it is independent even of the child's own waiting and longing to be released from pain.

The tenacious will to live is in every person, not only in children. It is even there in the elderly. They may be on the threshold of eternity. They may be completely ready to go, even longing for God to free them from their suffering. Yet when their time comes, when their body has given up and begun to disintegrate, they still go on fighting for life and cannot let go of the earth.

A few months ago a baby girl with serious congenital problems was born to a young couple in our church. Carmen has undergone numerous large and small operations since her birth, but to hold her when she is free from pain, to experience her radiant smiles, her cooing, and her joyful little soul stretching out to yours, is to feel the presence of a deep mystery that dwells in every one of us. This mystery is the primeval life-force of the soul which is there in even the frailest, most vulnerable body. It was not put there by the child's parents, nor by some coincidence, but by God, the creator and source of all life.

What a comfort this is to the believing mother, burdened by thoughts of an uncertain future or of the hardships that might one day face her child! God is with every child who suffers. Often this may seem too difficult to believe – even impossible. Why should our child, why should we, have to bear the burden of pain? Why does God give us a child to love and then take him or her away from us again? How can our grief possibly serve any purpose?

Even though no one can answer such deep questions satisfactorily, we know that none of us is exempt from suffering. If we can accept suffering – if we can open ourselves to it, even without understanding it – we can allow it to change us and, in doing so, give it meaning. We must believe that suffering can lead to faith, and to compassion for others who suffer.

Children, more than adults, often have a natural inclination to faith because they are so close to God. When we experience the faith of a child – indeed, whenever we sense faith in anyone at any time – we should be careful not to hinder it, but nurture it so that it may become a foundation on which to face future storms. My father writes:

> Children are closer than anyone else to the heart of Jesus, and he points to them as an example for us...The fact that children have to suffer is very strange. It is as if they are bearing someone else's guilt, as if they are suffering because of the fall of creation. In a way they seem to be paying the wages of sin – even though it is sin in which they have taken no active part as yet...Perhaps the suffering of children has a close connection with the greatest suffering ever endured: God's suffering, Christ's suffering for lost creation...The suffering of a child always has great significance.[22]

EMMY MARIA

My parents lost their first child, Emmy Maria, in 1938, due to a severe kidney problem. She was three months old. Obviously, the rest of us children never knew her, yet her short life had a deep significance for all of us. Both my father and my mother grew up with a view of life prevalent among the German youth of their day: the belief that everything that happens in creation has a deeper meaning, and even if we cannot discern that meaning, we should have reverence for creation and for the creator of all life.

Emmy Maria's short life deepened this outlook and had a profound effect not only on them but on our whole family and on the people around us. It was as if she fulfilled a divine task for us all. The following passages, quoted from a diary my parents kept during her sickness and the days before and after her death, may help other parents who face a similar situation.

It was quite extraordinary what such a small child could feel and notice, and how we could tell what she felt. It became clearer and clearer what her little soul was going through, and what she had to communicate to us. As her body grew weaker, it became more and more strongly an expression of her soul. That became powerfully clear to us in the hour of her death.

The last few days our child was given to live among us were hard for the human heart to bear, yet extremely great and powerful, filled with promise because of the nearness of Christ.

It was remarkable that each time we interceded for Emmy Maria and gathered ourselves inwardly, the powers of death withdrew, and she revived. Whereas before she lay there apathetic and unresponsive, with half-open eyes, shallow breath, and a very weak pulse, she would suddenly open her eyes, look at us, cry, and drink, moving her hands and turning her head when she was gently touched: she would come back to consciousness. Sometimes such a transformation came within seconds.

There was a special atmosphere of love in her room. It went out from her and filled the whole house, and united us in special love to each other...

We took turns watching by her. It was a hard fight, and

she had to suffer a great deal. It was a struggle with death, so real that it seemed incredible that such a tiny baby could take it up...

Emmy Maria gave us so much joy. Sometimes she would cry for hunger; then, when we fed her, she would smack her lips and suck for pleasure until she had swallowed her 20 grams from a dropper. We could tell that she felt happy to be with us at home. Sometimes she would smile in her sleep, and then her little mouth would widen...On awakening she would stretch and straighten herself and reach her hands up out of the covers.

In the last days there were some very critical moments. Her little face grew thinner and thinner, her eyes got bigger and bigger, and more and more expressive. Her little neck was so very thin...Again and again we held on to faith and trusted that a miracle could still be given; that she might be healed. Then at other times we wished that if it was not God's will for her to live, he might take her to himself soon and relieve her frail little body of its terrible torment and suffering.

Just before the end our little one opened her eyes wide, wider than they had ever been in her life. Then, with a clear, shining, otherworldly gaze, she looked at both of us for a long time. There was no sorrow and no suffering left in those eyes, but a message from the other world, a message of joy. Her eyes were not dull and clouded but bright and shining. She could not tell us anything in words, of course, but her eyes bore witness to the heavenly splendor and unspeakable joy there is with Christ. With this gaze, our dearly beloved child took leave of us. We shall never forget those radiant eyes.

MARK JOHN

Several years ago another couple at one of our communities lost a son to cancer. The youngest child in the family, Mark John was a sunny, lovable three-year-old. His story, as recorded by his parents in their diary, illustrates in a wonderful way how the trusting faith of a suffering child can work redemptively in those around him:

> The doctors at Yale-New Haven proposed that Mark John be transferred to a hospital in New York City for rigorous chemotherapy along with some other new treatment still at the experimental stage. When we asked them how much it would help Mark John, they could only say that at best it might prolong his life two to eight months, and at the price of his becoming deathly sick. When pressed, they reluctantly admitted that he would suffer terribly; in fact, he could die from the treatment itself...
>
> We decided that we would rather have our child at home, close to us, than in a hospital, even if he would live a little longer. It was an agonizing decision, but we know that God alone has all our lives in his hand, and especially the life of our little boy.
>
> Daily Mark John became weaker and weaker. After a few weeks, Heinrich, the elder of our church, suggested that we bring him to a service where we could lay him into the arms of the church and intercede for him. We knew Jesus could heal him, but we also knew that he might want to have him back...
>
> The service was very simple. Heinrich spoke about how Jesus loves all the children of the world, and then we prayed

that God's will would be done, and that we would be ready to accept it.

Easter had special meaning for us, thinking of Jesus' suffering and deepest pain, his godforsakenness and need for help, and then the resurrection and its unbelievable promise to every believer. Mark John was surely a believer. He believed like Jesus told us to – like a child.

On Easter morning his mother took him on a long walk in his wagon and talked to him about heaven and the angels and Jesus. She told him he would soon go to heaven, and that he should wait for us, and someday we would all be together again. He listened and nodded and sometimes said, "Yes." Later, when the rest of the family joined them, he pulled his big sister down to him and whispered joyfully, "Natalie, soon I'll get wings!"

Then Mark John lost his sight in one eye. He cried when he realized it. We were in such a tension: Would he be blind before Jesus came to take him? We longed so much that he might be spared that ordeal.

Once when he was lying on our bed between us, he asked us about the picture hanging on the wall opposite our bed – a painting of the Good Shepherd leaning over a cliff to rescue a lamb, with a bird of prey hovering over it. We knew a bird of prey was hovering over our little child too, but he was so unaware, so trusting. He grew thoughtful as he looked at the picture and asked us to tell him about it. We told him that Jesus was the Good Shepherd, and that we all are his lambs – also he. It was remarkable how he listened intently and seemed to understand…

By now he was eating hardly anything at all. He got thinner and thinner, and we feared he would starve. We wondered how long our other children could endure to see him suffer so much, as this illness slowly but terribly distorted and changed his dear face and body. Yet somehow, love showed us the way. All the children wanted to be with him. They accepted his suffering completely…

One day when we bent over him as he lay in his little wagon, he reached out his thin arms and cried pitifully, "I can't see, I can't see!" We said, "When you are in heaven – when your guardian angel comes and carries you to the arms of Jesus – you will be able to see again." But he could not be comforted. He asked, "When? When?" and we said, "Soon." He argued and said "No," so I had to insist, "I promise." Then he grew calm.

A day or two later, when we said goodnight to Mark John, he reached up and said, "I want to kiss you, Mommy," and gave her a healthy kiss. He kissed his mother first and then me. We were both so moved and happy because he hadn't asked for a kiss like that for several days: his little head turned towards his Mommy with his precious eyes that couldn't see any longer…

Often during the last days we talked with Mark John and told him that he was a brave boy, that we were very, very happy that he had come to us, and that he always was a good boy. On two occasions he answered us very emphatically, shaking his little head and saying, "No, no." It distressed us. We didn't know what he meant, but in retrospect we feel that maybe he just wanted to remind us that he was also sometimes naughty, and that he was sorry for it.

On the last day he vomited blood; Milton, our doctor, turned to us and said, "Soon." Then we sang a song that we had sung many times during the last days: "We shall walk through the valley of the shadow of death." When we came to the refrain, "Jesus himself shall be our leader," Mark John said distinctly, "Yes, yes, yes."

Mark John was given incredible strength in his last hours. Several times he said, "Up, up!" We asked him if he wanted to go up to heaven, and he said, "Yes." At one point we said, "Good-bye, Mark John," and he said, "Not yet." That was about an hour before he was taken.

A little later, as we were bending over him, he suddenly said, "Laugh!"

"What, Mark John?"

"Laugh!"

"But why should we laugh, darling?"

"Because," was the short but emphatic answer. And then, while we were still trying to grasp it, he repeated, *"Please, laugh!"*

Then we said, "Good-bye, Mark John," and he said, "Bye-bye." We told him we would see him again soon, because for him in eternity it will be very soon. Then he lifted both his arms and stretched them up and pointed with both fingers toward heaven, and his eyes looked and saw – his blind eyes that couldn't see any longer on this earth, but already saw beyond our world – and called out, "Not two! One!" He repeated this two or three times. "Not two! One!" He saw two angels coming to fetch him, and we had always told him only about one.

Then he turned toward his mother and said distinctly and tenderly, "Mommy, Mommy." Then he said "Papa, Papa." It was as if he wanted to unite us very closely. And then, in that dear and characteristic way of his, nodding his head, he said, "Mark John, Mark John." It was as if he had heard Jesus calling his name, and was repeating it. We had never heard him say his own name like that before. We bent over him, and then two more times he lifted up his arms and pointed to heaven with those thin arms that had been too weak even to lift a cup to his mouth for days.

Then, fighting for breath, he called out, "Mommy, Mommy, Mommy, Mommy." Ellen talked to him softly and reassuringly...He was still breathing heavily but we could not feel his little heart any more. And then came the last precious breath and the agonizing sigh. Death had taken his body, but his soul was victorious and free. We called to our darling little boy, "Mark John, Mark John!" But he was gone. Milton said, "It is all over now. His soul is free and with God. He has no more pain." We asked, "Are you really sure?" And Milton said, "I am sure beyond doubt." It was between 3 and 4 a.m....

As we look back on that night, we can see now that Mark John was slowly moving into another world. He went trustingly, even happily. It was as if we were standing before the gates to eternity, and we could take him that far, but then we would have to leave him. He would go in, and we would have to wait.

CHAPTER SIXTEEN

The Special Child

IN MARK 8:34 Jesus says, "If anyone wants to be my follower, he must deny himself, shoulder his cross and follow me." Christ's words were addressed not only to the people of his time, but also to us today: each of us who desires to follow him must be willing to carry the burden laid on us by God. Because the cross each person carries is different, we sometimes tend to look at others and compare our lot with theirs. When envy makes us dissatisfied with ourselves, we look at others and think, for instance, "He (or she) is so athletic" – or articulate, or musical, or easygoing – and we begin to wonder whether the person we envy has any cross at all to bear.

Every man, woman, and child has his or her own burden to carry. Even the Apostle Paul had a "thorn in his flesh." He asked God to remove it, but God answered him, "My grace is sufficient for you, for my power is made perfect in weakness" (2 Cor. 12:8). If we accept the grace God gives us, we will be able to bear the heaviest cross. And, strange as it may seem, it can even become a blessing.

The discovery that a newborn child is disabled can be a deeply shaking experience for any couple. Unfortunately it is common for some, in their shock, to assume that they have done something wrong. I would advise parents to give no room to such thoughts. Rather, turn to God and seek to see the situation as from his eyes – as a blessing that can lead you closer to each other and to God. He comes close to us through every child, but especially through children with disabilities.

We cannot understand the mystery of life and death; we do not know why one baby is born mentally or physically disabled while the next is perfect and healthy. Yet we do know that everything that happens, good or evil, has a purpose. And we know that God can turn any affliction into a blessing if we humbly accept whatever he sends.

Today, with the wide availability of sophisticated prenatal tests, fetal abnormalities are often discovered early in pregnancy. More and more, doctors subsequently advise abortion, arguing that this is in the best interest of both child and parents and that, even if such disabled babies are carried to term, their survival may not be guaranteed. Pope John Paul II writes:

> The point has been reached where the most basic care, even nourishment, is denied to babies born with serious handicaps or illnesses. The contemporary scene, moreover,

is becoming even more alarming by reason of the propos-
als, advanced here and there, to justify even infanticide,
following the same arguments used to justify the right to
abortion…

We see…the spread of euthanasia – disguised and sur-
reptitious, or practiced openly and even legally – justified
by the utilitarian motive of avoiding costs which bring no
return and which weigh heavily on society. Thus it is proposed to eliminate malformed babies…

A life which would require greater acceptance, love,
and care is considered useless, or held to be an intolerable
burden, and is therefore rejected.[23]

Clearly, the specter of Nazi Germany and its state-sponsored
program of euthanasia still casts its shadow over our era. Let
us hope that today, in a society that places ever greater
emphasis on achievement, assertiveness, independence,
strength, and competitive success, we never forget the lessons that the disabled and the weak can teach us. Let us
allow their weakness and vulnerability to challenge our
self-confidence and inspire us to a deeper love and commitment. Christ comes to us in the form of a stranger, a beggar,
an angel. Why should he not also come in the form of
a handicapped child?

God has a specific purpose or task in mind for every person born on this earth. Everyone, even if he or she lives for
only a few minutes, brings us a certain message from God.
None of us can presume to know exactly what this message
is. All the same, the message is there, if only we open our

hearts to it. Jean Vanier* points out that the weak "seem to break down the barriers of powerfulness, of wealth, of ability, and of pride; they pierce the armor the human heart builds to protect itself; they reveal Jesus Christ God hides himself in them." He goes on to say that handicapped children especially have a mysterious power: with their tiny hands they can "slip through the bars of the prison of egoism." [24]

Tragically, many parents of disabled children have never had their hearts opened to these truths. All too often they are either impatient, even intolerant, or else overly protective. They have been hurt in their family pride; they regard their child as a disappointment. They feel dishonored and ashamed. Neighbors, relatives, and friends often aggravate the situation with insensitive remarks, as do the family doctors and therapists who suggest that the child be "put away" in an institution. The suffering of both parents and child is often appalling.

How different things would be if we saw special children first as gifts to be received with extra gratefulness and love, rather than as burdens! When Alan, the first child of a young Bruderhof couple, was born several months ago, it was soon clear that he was no ordinary child. Probably deaf and blind (it is too early to be completely certain) he also suffers from various abnormalities of the brain and may never walk or talk.

At a special service where we welcomed him into our

---

* Jean Vanier, author, pastor, and founder of L'Arche, a community movement that ministers to people with disabilities.

church community, Jonathan, Alan's father, expressed his feeling that it was even a blessing to have received such a child – a little being through whom he and his wife might learn more about love and compassion, also for others who suffer. He spoke of the joy of watching Alan's personality develop in spite of his severe handicaps. Various others shared thoughts, too, about the possible meaning of God's sending parents a severely disabled son or daughter: perhaps the little life will reveal some aspect of the gospel, some redemptive mystery not otherwise revealed through a normal child.

Sometimes the prospect of a disabled child is more than a couple is able to face without at least some struggle. In my experience, even the strongest parents will need to be supported as much as possible, and they should not be made to feel guilty when they accept (or seek) help. Those of us who do not have to cope with the added burden of a child with special needs should offer our support where we can in practical ways, for instance by taking the child into our home for a night or a weekend to let his or her parents relax and find new strength.

At the Bruderhof we have had children with Down syndrome, Prader Willi syndrome, and other serious handicaps over the years. All of them – Heidi, Lisa, Duane, Joanna, and Iris, to name a few of the ones with us at present – are a gift and blessing to their families, their peers, and the larger community; and all of them a living witness to the power of childlikeness and joy.

Miriam, who passed away in 1992 at the age of twenty-eight, was born with multiple crippling physical handicaps that repeated surgery was unable to alleviate. Nonetheless, her brightness and *joie d'vivre* touched countless lives. Frail and severely crippled, her determination to do what she could for herself and for others lasted to her final breath.

Sonja, who is fully incapacitated and needs twenty-four-hour care, was born in perfect health but left helpless by meningitis at the age of five months. Despite frequent suggestions by social workers to have Sonja institutionalized when she was a child, her parents and siblings wouldn't hear of it. Now, at thirty-eight, she is still part of her family and community and continues to call forth and respond to the loving care of those around her. As her mother says, "We think there is something special in Sonja. She has never consciously sinned, and must be very close to God. We always feel challenged to love her more."

Sasha, a young Russian man who was born without arms, was given into our care when he was sixteen in the hope that he could be fitted with prostheses. He had taught himself to be largely independent by using his feet to do what most people do with their hands, but the unnatural positions he was forced to repeat daily had severely curved his spine, and he lived in continuous pain. Despite tremendous odds – Sasha hardly knew a word of English when he arrived in the United States – his pluck and enthusiasm have stood him in good stead. Now, after months of research, surgery, and therapy, he is in the process of obtaining his prostheses.

Given the special needs of children with mental and physical disabilities, it is easy to see why parents are tempted to treat them differently from other children: to set no boundaries, to give into every whim, to spoil them. Yet to pamper such children is the greatest disservice one can do them, for it limits their entire future – their physical and mental development, and their emotional independence.

All children need the warmth of physical affection, and disabled children need it perhaps even more than others. But they should not be babied with constant hugs, kisses, and treats. Rather, they should be lovingly guided and encouraged to use their abilities to the fullest. This is not to say that they should be pushed to perform or to take on responsibilities beyond their capabilities. All the same, it is amazing what a loving environment and proper care and handling can do. In our work with the disabled, especially through Rifton, the Bruderhof's line of physical therapy equipment, we have experienced time and again how a combination of therapy and education can help the most incapacitated child toward mobility, independence, and most important, toward self-respect and a feeling of worth.

In concluding this section, I would like to share the stories of two special children, Bobby and Louisa. The first was written by Bobby's mother, Yvonne, a good friend over many years. The second was written by Louisa's parents, Dick and Lois Ann (fellow members of the Bruderhof) and her sister Rebekah.

BOBBY

In 1956, when our Bobby was born, there were no programs for retarded children. We felt very lost and knew nothing about Down syndrome or mental retardation. In our anguish we asked God for help and strength. We realize, as we look back, that God held us and led us right from the beginning. As we learned about our little son, we loved him all the more. We started to meet with other parents of special children. We found ourselves involved in helping to get programs and classes started. Most important, the love we felt for Bobby and our three little girls bonded us closer and closer together as a family. Bobby was a complete joy and gave unconditional love through all his life – even when he was very sick just before he died. His open friendliness to all with whom he came in contact made new friends for us all! When our girls married, our three sons-in-law became loving brothers to Bobby, and the bond in our family grew even stronger. What fun he had with them, roughhousing as only boys can do! I can still see them rolling together on a lawn full of leaves and tossing a ball back and forth.

Bobby was called into eternity in 1982. We had such a deep ache in our hearts, and missed him so very, very much. But we could only give grateful thanks to God for giving us this very dear and special boy to love and care for during those twenty-five years.

LOUISA

Louisa came to our family as a gift from God on April 7, 1967. Neither of us had any idea how she would develop or what she would be able to do, and as she slowly grew in her own way, we noted each new thing she could do with special joy. From the first day of her life, she was fully accepted by everyone in our family (she was our tenth child of eleven) and community, and we can never be grateful enough for the nurturing warmth and joy that surrounded her. It continued to surround her to her last breath.

Louisa had Down syndrome, yet she was completely accepted as one of the crowd by her age group. From early childhood on she was surprisingly responsive, and she loved her playmates as much as they loved her. In many ways Louisa was no different from other children: usually she was happy and contented, but on occasion she could be demanding, selfish, and stubborn.

In her early years we made the mistake of giving her too much leeway, but over the years we learned, especially with the help of her teachers, that she needed the same guidance and correction that her peers did. Her emotional responses might have been more extreme than theirs, but it did her no good to be treated with extra lenience. In fact, we observed that making extra allowances for her, at least in terms of her behavior, only added to the burdens she already had. When an inappropriate idea or fascination needed to be redirected, for instance, we learned to give her a straight word and bring her back to reality. Just as for any other child, there had to be boundaries. The basis of the relationship had to be genuine, not superficially cheerful or motivated by pity.

Though academically a slow learner, Louisa learned to read, write, sew, and knit; one year her embroidery even won the grand prize at the county fair. By the end of elementary school she had learned to jump rope and to swim. From very early on – two or three years – she responded to music; at eight she knew numerous songs by heart and sang them on pitch. She also learned to play simple tunes on the recorder and a small-size violin.

We tried to encourage and stretch Louisa in as many ways as we could, but we always felt it would be unloving (and even dangerous) to push her to become someone she wasn't. Our feelings were confirmed when a close friend of hers, a girl her age with Down syndrome, was given her own apartment and expected to look after herself entirely. The girl had made impressive progress in the months before this, it is true, but the final step to independence was too much for her, and she suffered a complete breakdown.

It was always clear to us that Louisa, who thrived on community life, would never be able to cope with such a situation. Her gifts lay in her sensitivity to others, even complete strangers, her infectious happiness, her ability to share another's joy as if it were her own, and her heartfelt response to even the smallest kindness. As with other special children, it didn't take much to encourage her.

Racism and social injustice concerned Louisa greatly, and sometimes, when she was with a black person, she would put her hand next to his or hers and say, "Black and white together." In the last years, as her heart condition caused her own skin to darken from poor circulation, she would do this with another white person and say the same thing. The civil rights song "We shall overcome" became her theme song; to her it referred just as much to her own struggle for life as to the fight for racial justice.

Three or four years before she died, when she was in her mid-twenties, she entered a Bruderhof essay contest on the issue of Israeli-Palestinian relations. After enlisting support to put her thoughts on paper, she turned in the following entry:

> ...The Palestinians throw stones because the Jewish people take away their homes. But...the Jewish people are fighting for their homeland. The problem is: both are in the same place. They should forgive each other with loving hearts...All the nations should come together in peace and unity and sing "We shall overcome" and shake hands and hug one another. The heavenly kingdom will come on earth. Jesus loves the Palestinians and the Israelis. They will both come to the kingdom of God...

Louisa was born with an inoperable heart defect that became more and more serious the older she got. All the same, she rarely complained, and when someone asked her how she was feeling, she always answered, "Me? I'm fine!"

In the last year-and-a-half of her life, her condition gradually worsened, and especially in the last six months her heart grew much weaker. She refused to think of her

sickness as anything serious, however, and resisted any at
tempts to treat her like a patient. She was determined to
lead an active social life as long as possible. Even in the
last weeks of her life she spent time writing cards, drawing
pictures, and knitting a scarf for one of her friends.

Right to the last evening before she passed away she
held on to life: she would wake out of sleep and say, "I am
thinking about *life!*" Her happy chuckle was one of the
last things to go. She did not want tears and sadness around
her, but she understood the pain we felt and reached out
to each person around her. She reassured us again and
again, saying, "Don't worry, I'm just resting."

Louisa's humor, even in the most difficult moments,
moved us very deeply. On her last afternoon she told a
visitor who asked her how she was doing, "Don't worry,
it's nothing serious. Think about Charlie Chaplin." Her
joy in music, too, stayed with her right to the end. She
always loved Beethoven's *Ninth Symphony* and responded
to its message of joy very personally. In the last two days,
when the energy to communicate this in words gradually
left her, she gave us the thumbs-up sign many times.

At about 3:15 on the morning of Louisa's last day,
February 13, 1996, her final struggle began. She was wide
awake, looking directly into each of our faces. Her soul
was ready to go, but it took a great fight. Each breath was
a milestone on her journey upward. We stood by her,
assuring her that God's angels were with her and she would
soon be victorious. The tape recorder was playing one
of her favorite pieces – a children's Easter cantata – and
during the last song, just at the words "Arise, fling wide
the gates of Paradise," she took her last breath and went.

It was a victory: at last she was free, called home to the upper world where there is only love, peace, and eternal joy.

Special children – whether mentally or physically disabled, deformed, autistic, or different in any other way – should never be rejected, either when conceived, when born, or when they reach adulthood. Like Bobby and Louisa, they can bring us far more than we might ever expect. Their lives are a clear testimony to the fact that each person, no matter how weak and vulnerable, is a gift from God, not least by reminding us of our own weakness and dependence on him.

CHAPTER SEVENTEEN

Adoption

ASIDE FROM THE THOUSANDS of unborn children whose lives are snuffed out by abortion every year, thousands more are born but then left unwanted on our doorsteps. Some are rejected by parents who cannot face the demands of feeding yet another mouth; others are abandoned because they are malformed or crippled. In recent years, increasing numbers have been left in garbage cans and dumpsters by teenagers who cannot cope with the consequences of their sexual activity, or by adult mothers who are abusive, addicted to crack, or unable to survive economically.

Obviously, it is the biological parents of such children who bear the greatest obligation toward them. Yet at the same time, the abandonment of babies and small children is an indictment on all of us. We bear a guilt too – those of us whose privileged middle-class lifestyles have, at least in part, created the ghettos where every card is stacked against even those parents who do try to raise their children responsibly.

One concrete way in which we can fight the rising tide of child abandonment is by encouraging young mothers to carry their babies to term, and then helping them to find adoptive parents. There are couples, also in our Bruderhof communities, to whom the joy of having their own children is denied by medical circumstances such as infertility. Many wait for years to adopt a newborn baby but are ultimately unsuccessful because of the endless tangle of legal requirements and the exorbitant fees that accompany the adoption process.

Although there are tens of thousands of children waiting for foster homes, it can still take years of waiting and thousands of dollars to adopt a child. In some cases the selection process is slowed because children do not meet the high standards or particular wishes of prospective parents. Then, too, many government requirements are justified to protect babies and foster parents from illegal adoption agencies, some of whom make millions of dollars in stolen profits each year. All the same, it is clear that something drastic needs to be done to make adoption easier and less economically burdensome, even if safely regulated. Perhaps the trend toward private adoption agencies will show itself to be a partial answer.

Raising an adopted child is rarely an easy task. Many of the children put up for adoption have been victims of abuse and neglect, and even when this is not the case, the circumstances of their birth may leave them scarred in soul and spirit.

Further discussion of adoption is beyond the scope of this book, but let me leave the reader with the following thoughts. Though written more than a century ago, they still hold true:

Whoever adopts children must accept them with all their ingratitude; otherwise it will not go well. To take in children and expect thanks is unnatural and not right. As a rule, it will go badly. Children never show special thanks to those who feed and clothe them, apart from showing love the way children do. They take it quite for granted that we don't let them go hungry or naked, also that we don't do just the minimum for them if they see that we could do a little more. That is theirs by rights, whoever cares for them.

Many who adopt children, however, think that such children should acknowledge and feel awed by the fact that people who do not owe them anything (if that is true at all) take them in out of compassion. But that is just what they do *not* feel, so do not demand it of them. Love them without expecting thanks, even if they cause you a lot of trouble; you have to accept them along with their naughtiness. They will feel that, and will love you for it, but without words.

Often foster children are given what they need, but without love, and they are made to feel this even in words. It hurts them deeply and can even give rise to hatred in their hearts...

Foster children do not want to have fewer privileges than the children they live with; they have a sharp eye, and if they see differences, it hurts them terribly. Why is that? They are simply children, and they do not see why one child should have more than another.

If you adopt children, adopt them fully so they can be free to simply be children and can make any childlike demand of you.[25]

Finally, let us remember the wonderful promise of Jesus that "whoever receives a child in my name, receives me" (Mt. 18:5). Surely this applies to every couple, to every man or woman who takes a child into his or her home.

CHAPTER EIGHTEEN

Children and Sin

GIVEN THE CURRENT CLIMATE of extreme permissiveness, some readers will no doubt raise their eyebrows at the heading of this chapter. Children get into trouble, they'll agree, but do they – can they – really *sin?*

Let me say this: Despite the inclination of every human being toward sin, it seems to me that if anyone will enter the kingdom of heaven, it is little children. Surely they are far closer to God than we are. On the other hand, I believe it is a mistake to regard children as naturally good, to see them through rose-colored glasses and excuse everything they do as merely childish. (I am speaking here not of two- and three-year-olds, but of kindergarten and grade school children.)

My grandfather Eberhard Arnold writes.

There can be no doubt that even the smallest child bears within him something from his parents that burdens him. And yet a small child is in quite a different situation from us adults with regard to this inherited inclination toward evil. The basic difference is that the child has not yet made a conscious decision for evil. The legacy of godlessness and antisocial forces, of the bad traits and bad experiences of his parents and forebears, is a burden on him. But it has not yet matured into deed. That is the difference between children and adults.[26]

When children do wrong, we must remember that it is rarely with the degree of intention we adults tend to assume. Children almost never mean things the way adults do, even when they commit the same wrongs. Nevertheless, it is an error to conclude from this that children are not susceptible to evil. They are, and they must be helped to choose right over wrong again and again. Their will is still completely free, and because of this they must not be left unprotected to fall prey to evil, but won over for the good.

The best way to do this is to build a relationship of mutual love and trust. Human nature being what it is, however, discipline will still be necessary as well. Certainly harshness or cruelty of any kind toward children is always wrong, but so is permissiveness. If we love God with all our hearts and long to guide our children to him, our relationship with them will contain the salt that true love demands.

When a child has done wrong – when he or she has taken something that belongs to someone else, been disobedient, lied, or hurt another child – discipline him or her as soon as possible. When this has been done, forgive him or her fully and move on to make a new beginning. Long-drawn-out punishments are never helpful.

Because each parent (and each child) is so different, I hesitate to advise a specific form of discipline. Sometimes it may be best to deprive the child (temporarily, of course) of something he or she enjoys; in other instances "time out" will be more effective; in still others a good row will be necessary. The main thing is that love motivates the discipline in every case, not impatience or anger.

In fighting sinful tendencies in children, it is critical that we remove the pitfalls caused by the sin in our own hearts and lives. True love for children means reverence for them, and this reverence has its roots in the love we have for God. When we have true reverence for God, for ourselves, and for our children, they too will find the same.

When children show off, for instance, or bully other children, we cannot only admonish them. We need to ask ourselves why they feel the need to make themselves important. Is their behavior a cry for attention or a reaction to some lack of love on our part? And if we cannot clearly discern whether or not they have consciously decided to do wrong, let us not jump to conclusions.

Never try to catch children in the act and then use your evidence to prove their guilt. That is an act of moral violence. If you distrust children and read bad motives into their behavior, you weaken them instead of strengthening them. Likewise, never make children overly aware of their bad impulses. You will destroy not only their natural freedom and self-confidence, but also their trust in you.

No matter how many times your children get into trouble, forgive them. Who is to say that the tendencies you are struggling to overcome in them are not reflections of the same tendencies in yourself? "Forgive, so your Father in heaven will forgive you" (Mark 11:25). Never label them or be tempted to give them up as "hopeless." Lack of hope is a lack of love. If you truly love your children, you will not throw up your hands in despair. Even at the end of the roughest day, you will not lose joy in them.

Lastly, don't neglect prayer. In *Baby and Child Care,* a book that influenced a whole generation of Americans, author Dr. Benjamin Spock assures parents that they know more than they think they know, and implies that when faced with the bewildering array of questions that inevitably arise in child rearing, they should trust their own God-given abilities. Parents do need to trust their judgment if they are to be effective, but they also need to realize that there is more to parenthood than techniques and methods. In searching for the best way to guide children, especially when they have done wrong, humble parents will turn first to God for help.

WILLFULNESS

As sayings go, "Little children, little problems; big children, big problems" might be dismissed as an old cliché. Yet the fact remains that most clichés contain plenty of truth. Undisciplined three- and four-year-olds will grow into uncontrollable teenagers and adults. I do not mean to suggest by this that parents should regard their children as potential problems, but simply that when they become so headstrong that they cannot control themselves, it should be seen as a serious matter and be taken care of. More than a few battle-weary parents will be able to attest that one child's self-will can disrupt a whole family.

Regardless of how small a child is, there is no reason why he or she cannot learn to say "I'm sorry" after having done something wrong – and mean it. Humility takes a lifetime to learn, and parents who fail to instill it in their children when they are small will discover that it becomes more and more difficult as they grow older. The will of a small child may be guided with relative ease, but the will of a teenager can only be broken with strenuous effort.

SELFISHNESS AND JEALOUSY

Selfishness and jealousy are not the same in children as they are in adults. Children are the center of their own little universes: they see the whole world around them from the perspective of their yard or playroom, and they own it. When they take something to themselves enthusiastically, it is not because they are selfish or possessive in the usual sense of the word, but because they have become absorbed in it. Such natural self-centeredness is not in itself wrong. All the same, every child needs help to overcome it as he or she grows older.

Generosity, like anything else, is learned by example. If you as parent or educator are not generous yourself, don't expect your children to share a toy or treat, or to give up something they are looking forward to. But if you refrain from interfering when they impulsively decide, for instance, to give away a best toy (even if you had just bought it, and it was expensive), they will feel your tacit approval for their generosity; they may even be less possessive about their other things in the future.

When a small child is jealous, help him (or her) to put himself in the shoes of the person he envies. Point out to him, for example, that the reason this or that child is getting all the attention is because it's her birthday today, and remind him that he had a party on his birthday, too. If he persists in making envious comparisons, remind him of all the children who never get anything, or of the many children in the world who don't even have parents to love them. In most cases, this will be enough to address the problem. If it isn't, appeal to him by helping him to realize that even in the most ideal situations, life is never a level field; often, things simply are not "fair." On the other hand, don't forget the effects of a child's personality and place in the family. Is he or she the oldest child? the youngest? an only child? Don't show favoritism.

When children are selfish or quarrelsome, intervene in a positive way, helping them learn to work out their differences in friendship and love. On the whole, you will find that they have an amazing capacity for compassion. Always remember that your main focus should be on affirming this capacity, not on fighting their inclination to selfishness. In this way, they will begin to grasp the meaning of the two greatest commandments of Jesus: "Love God with all your heart, mind, and soul," and "Love your neighbor as yourself."

DISHONESTY

When parents discover that a child has been dishonest, it is important to get to the facts of what happened, to encourage the child to face up to them, and then to help him or her apologize. It is rarely good to probe into all the possible motives; in fact, great harm has been done to children in this way. God knows a child's temptations and motivations, but he also sees much more – the deepest longings of the child's heart.

Often, embarrassment or shame will cause a child to wriggle out of something by means of a half-truth. If he (or she) is really afraid of the consequences of what he has done, he may tell an outright lie. None of this should surprise us. Don't adults lie for the same reasons? The heart of the issue is this: children sometimes lack the courage to admit their wrongdoings and must be helped to regain it. They must also be helped to feel genuinely sorry both for their initial misdeed and their dishonesty.

If you are relatively sure a child has lied, but not completely certain, don't press him or her to admit anything. Accept their answer with something like: "Okay, you say you didn't do it. But if you have anything more to tell us, you can always come back." In my experience, children will respond to this suggestion; they will even wake their parents in the middle of the night to admit a lie, because their conscience bothers them.

Again, never force children into making a confession. That will only scare them into telling further lies in the future. Sooner or later the truth will come out. When it does, let them know how happy you are, and share their joy in having made a clean slate of it.

Between the ages of three and eight (or even ten), some children let their imagination run wild and tell their playmates, teachers, or parents stories they firmly believe are true. Some children will even act out imaginary situations. At one of our Bruderhof schools, a video on water safety resulted in a six-year-old putting on a drowning act the next day. The teacher accused her of crying wolf, but the girl insisted that she was neither pretending to drown nor trying to scare her teacher. Most likely that was true: she was simply acting out what she had seen, perhaps to rid herself of her own anxiety after the film.

If a young child acts in this way, don't punish her, but exercise understanding and patience. She is not lying and should not be dealt with as though she were. She is simply expressing her inability to distinguish between reality and imagination. With older children, tackle such behavior, but don't make too much of it. Simply guide the child to recognize the actual facts of the situation.

Mockery

Silliness is a common trait among younger children and usually erupts when they are aimless, bored, or looking for attention. In general, it marks the natural transition from early childhood to preschool and is nothing to be worried about. At times, however, it may lead to disrespect and mockery, and then it will demand firm inner guidance.

Games such as making silly faces may start out harmlessly enough, but when they escalate, they can become problematic, especially when they take on a rude or even nasty edge. The same is true of "bathroom talk," where the line between childish naiveté and indecency is often quickly crossed and it will be necessary to help the child: "I don't want you talking like that."

Mockery among children should be taken seriously. Mostly a sign of irreverence and disrespect toward others, it often develops into a lack of reverence for God. Name-calling and teasing is bad enough children, like adults, can be extraordinarily cruel to each other – but when it leads to imitating another person's mannerisms or physical characteristics in an unkind way, it should never be tolerated or brushed off as a childish form of amusement.

In tackling the problem of mockery in children, it is important that parents and teachers examine themselves first. Children are extremely perceptive to the atmosphere around them, and they will never fail to notice hypocrisy, especially religious hypocrisy.

When I was growing up, my parents took the slightest hint of mockery in us children very seriously. Like boys and girls anywhere, we sometimes mocked adults whose peculiarities we found "funny." I can still remember how my friends and I used to ridicule Nikolaus, a simple-minded man who stuttered, and Günther, an extremely tall, rather academically-inclined librarian. We thought we were being clever, but our parents failed to see the humor. They saw our cruelty for what it was and would not tolerate it.

Sexual Curiosity *

In the history of religious groups all over the world, especially in the more conservative traditions, children and teenagers have often been treated harshly because of perceived sexual sin. The Bruderhof is no exception. Although such moral strictness is almost always well-meant, it is a terrible trap to fall into, and it can cause great and even irreparable harm. Froebel writes:

> There…are men of mischief among educators…[who] are the first to bring guilt upon a child, who, though not totally innocent, is yet without guilt, for they give him motives and incentives which were as yet unknown to him; they make his actions bad…Children, especially boys, are often punished by parents and other adults for faults and misdemeanors they…learned from these very persons. Punishment…very often teaches children, or at least brings to their notice, faults of which they were previously wholly free.[27]

* See p. 122 below, "Sex Education."

In regard to the question of children and the sexual sphere, Froebel's last point is especially well taken. Never ask a child too many questions, and do not project your own adult ideas, feelings, and experiences onto a child's mind. Young children simply will go through periods of sexual curiosity that lead them to expose themselves and touch each other, and this must never be mistaken for sin. Children will also ask questions about sex, in which case parents should answer truthfully and without embarrassment, though not offering more information than they have been asked for.

If a child offends in the sexual area, discipline him (or her) as you see fit – unless he is a little child, in which case simply distract him – and move on. Because the child will instinctively feel that what he has done is wrong, he may lie; still, parents should be careful not to make too much of the matter. Determine what actually took place, and again, move on. Lengthy questioning will only draw his attention to the sexual area all the more.

When children are disciplined too harshly, the ultimate purpose of disciplining them – helping them to make a fresh start – is overshadowed by the discipline itself. As soon as a child recognizes that he or she has done wrong and shows a desire to make amends, forgive him or her immediately and completely. Once forgiven, a child's wrongdoing should never be mentioned again. It should be forgotten, and the child should be helped to move on joyfully

My parents, both educators, never tired of emphasizing what a great injustice it is to label children or adolescents for their misdeeds, especially in the sexual area. They said that it is always dangerous, in assessing childish "offenses," to draw hasty conclusions about the child's character and future development. It is far more constructive to help the child in question to find new interests.

In my experience, it is possible to find the way to the heart of any child by appealing to his or her conscience. Every child has an instinctive longing for a pure conscience, and we should support this longing.

CHAPTER NINETEEN

Building Character

W E LIVE IN A TIME when "anything goes"; when there is the widespread feeling that we must never stand up too strongly for our beliefs, because we may hurt someone who does not share them. Certainly it is not right to be intolerant of other people's convictions, or to force one's beliefs on them by buttonholing them or trying to coerce them in any other way. At the same time, the fact that very few of us have ever had to stand up for what we believe has left us spineless. Many of us lack the depth of commitment that comes with being tested.

How can parents raise children with moral backbone – children who are able, as they grow up, to hold on to their convictions? First and foremost, they must instill in them a sense of moral courage, which is, very simply, an attitude of confidence, determination, and perseverance. In his book *Freedom from Sinful Thoughts,* my father writes how a person's attitude to the difficulties of life determines his or her emotional well-being. This is just as true, of course, for children. They must learn to adopt an aggressive attitude to cold, heat, and fatigue, to apathy and indulgence, to fears, hurts, and disappointments.

Children need to learn to be plucky; they cannot dissolve in tears at every taunt or jeer. They must learn to withstand peer pressure and the humiliation of being despised for holding an unpopular idea. They must also realize that humility is no less vital to building character than the ability to think for oneself. It may take courage to hold an opposing viewpoint in a crowd of friends, but it takes just as much courage, if not more, to own up to a mistake or to admit defeat when one is wrong.

Clearly, the formation of character only begins in childhood and must continue as a lifelong process. Yet if parents lay a firm foundation for their children at home, set realistic goals for them, and live up to these goals themselves, they will not be disappointed. Foerster* says:

> A child is educated not by having lengthy talks about "big" things, but by patiently teaching him or her to carry out the smallest and most ordinary tasks properly. Character is formed through training in the smallest and mundane things, not in the "stream of the world."[28]

On a deeper level, a child's strength of character (or lack of it) will have a bearing on his or her readiness to suffer for the sake of a conviction. Given the measure of religious freedom

---

*Friedrich Wilhelm Foerster (1869–1966), German writer and educator.

we enjoy at present, some readers may find it strange even to raise this issue. Yet, as anyone who experienced the McCarthy era in this country will attest to, things can change quickly. Throughout history and right down to the present day, followers of almost every religion and ideology have had to endure periods of persecution.

The sooner our children realize that discipleship means suffering and hardship, the better equipped they will be for the future. I still remember how, as a child, I was deeply moved by a true story my parents read to me about a 16th-century miller's boy who was executed because he refused to recant his "heretical" beliefs[29] – and how it made me think for the first time about the whole issue of standing up for one's convictions. Although we should teach our children to live for the present and not burden them unduly with worries about the future, it will never hurt them to learn that faith does not preclude suffering.

Jesus did not promise his followers good times. The greater our faith, the greater the opposition we may have to face because of it.

CHAPTER TWENTY

Consideration
for Others

IT IS RELATIVELY EASY to raise children to be polite and to teach them good manners. It is much harder, but also much more important, to instill in them a genuine sensitivity to the perspectives and needs of others. True consideration is far more than a matter of manners. It means loving one's neighbor as oneself.

There are many ways to encourage children to think of others. Take them to buy flowers for a grandparent, help them to bake cookies for a friend's birthday, or bring them along to visit a lonely or elderly neighbor. As children learn to see beyond their own little worlds, they will discover the satisfaction of bringing joy to others.

In *The Heart of a Boy,* a collection of true stories by the Italian writer Edmondo de Amicis, the author illustrates the significance of consideration for others – and the value of peer pressure when it is channeled to a positive end – with incidents from his own life.[30] One chapter tells the story of Nelli, a hunchbacked boy, who is befriended by an older, stronger boy named Garrone. Nelli is thin and sickly and breathes with difficulty. On the first day of school, many of the boys laugh at him because he is a hunchback and beat him with their school bags. Nelli never retaliates. Nor does he tell his mother about it, because he doesn't want to cause her the pain of knowing that her son is the laughingstock of the school.

Then one day in gym class all the boys have to climb a greased pole:

> As soon as the boys saw Nelli take hold of the pole with those long, thin hands, many began to laugh. But Garrone crossed his big arms on his chest and shot such an expressive glance around, and made it so clearly understood that he was ready to stand up for Nelli, that they all stopped laughing at once.
>
> Nelli began to climb. He tried hard, poor little fellow; his face turned purple, he breathed heavily, the sweat ran down his forehead.
>
> The master said, "Come down!" but he wouldn't. He struggled and went on. I expected every minute to see him slip down, half dead. "Poor Nelli!"...
>
> In the meantime, [the other boys] were saying, "Up, up! Nelli, try! Once more! Courage!"
>
> And Nelli made one more violent effort, gave a groan, and found himself within two handbreadths of the cross bar near the top.
>
> "Bravo!" cried all the others. "Courage! Just one more

pull!" and there was Nelli holding the bar.

"Bravo!" said the master. "But that will do. Come down now."

But Nelli wanted to climb to the top like the others; and after a little effort he succeeded in getting his elbows on the bar, then his knees, and then his feet. Finally he stood upright, breathless and smiling, and looked at us.

We began to clap our hands, and then he looked into the street. I turned in that direction and…saw his mother, who was walking up and down the sidewalk, without daring to look.

Nelli came down, and we all made much of him. He was excited and rosy; his eyes were shining, and he did not look like the same boy.

Then at the close, when his mother came to meet him and…asked a little anxiously, "Well, my dear child, how did it go?" All the boys answered together, "He did well. He climbed like the rest of us. He is strong, you know. He is quick. He does things just like the others."

Then you should have seen the lady's delight! She wanted to thank us and couldn't. She shook hands with three or four…and carried her son away. And we watched them for a while, walking fast, perfectly happy, both of them talking and gesticulating.

Racism

Hatred toward people of a different race, color, or culture is a learned thing. Children are colorblind; left to themselves, they play happily together, oblivious of any differences in the shade of their skin. When they get older they will naturally begin to notice differences, yet even then their awareness will never be a matter of prejudice or hatred. Racism is present only among children whose self-awareness and awareness of others has been distorted by the adults around them.

Despite decades of discussion about equal rights for minorities, no real progress has been made. Racial bigotry and intolerance may be better masked, but they still define personal and public life to a great degree. At the Bruderhof, where we have a small but growing number of African-Americans, we are only just beginning to grasp the depth of the hurt and pain caused by racism. The psychological imprint of centuries of hatred and cruelty is almost beyond the comprehension of us who are white.

Whenever any form of racism – a narrow-minded view about interracial marriage, for instance – rears its head, we must point our children (and each other) away from the foolishness of human ideas about color, culture, and class. Most important, we must seek the love of God, who created us with all our differences, and show our children by our words and deeds that we are committed to striving for justice and brotherhood among all men and women on earth. For, as Dostoyevsky points out in *The Brothers Karamazov,* the sensitivity of children is so great that we often shape their attitudes without even knowing it:

> Every day and hour...see that your image is a seemly one. You pass by a little child, you pass by, spiteful, with ugly

words, with wrathful heart; you may not have noticed the child, but he has seen you, and your image, unseemly and ignoble, may remain in his defenseless heart. You don't know it, but you may have sown an evil seed in him, and it may grow...all because you did not foster in yourself an active, actively benevolent love.[31]

CHAPTER TWENTY-ONE

Sports and Play

IF EARLY CHILDHOOD is the most formative phase of life, play is surely its most important part. It is a beautiful thing to see a child thoroughly absorbed in his or her play; in fact, it is hard to think of a purer, more spiritual activity. Play brings joy, contentment, and complete detachment from the troubles of the day. Especially nowadays, in our hectic, time- and money-driven culture, the significance of play and the innocent relaxation of daydreaming that accompanies it cannot be emphasized enough.

Johann Christoph Blumhardt,* a father and grandfather of a large family, advised that parents should refrain from doing anything that might make a child unhappy by tearing him or her away from play – or that they should at least consider it carefully beforehand. He points out that children need to think for themselves and in their own way;

*Johann Christoph Blumhardt (1805–1880), German Lutheran pastor, father of Christoph Friedrich Blumhardt.

they need full scope to let their own imaginations work and to notice things for themselves: "that is their first school; they are teaching themselves, as it were. I often have the feeling that angels are around children...and that whoever is so clumsy as to disturb a child provokes his angel."[32]

When children are older, it is necessary to channel their energies to constructive ends, but it is also good, now and then, to let them do whatever they choose. Children will use their free time in a wide variety of ways. One will spend an entire afternoon reading in a tree; another will work on a favorite hobby; still another will find the greatest bliss simply in playing with a pet or a doll. Resist the temptation to constantly guide their interests. Let them play freely, and wherever possible, let the unstructured hours of the day present their own possibilities. "Free time" helps children learn to make choices and gives them the chance to develop individually.

Outdoor activities, whether circle games in the kindergarten or organized sports at the high school level, provide a good means for physical exercise and an outlet for energy. Equally important, they are good ground for learning teamwork and for experiencing the sense of well-being that comes from pushing oneself to one's physical limits. And they teach the importance of following rules, as even the apostle Paul noted (2 Tim. 2:5). There are other benefits, too: it has been observed, for instance, that athletic self-confidence often carries over to study habits. Froebel even says that a child who plays thoroughly, with determination, persevering until physical fatigue overcomes him or her, will surely be a thorough, determined adult, capable of self-sacrifice for others.[33]

With sports, as with any other field of activity, it is important to let every child grow in his or her own way. Football, basketball, softball, and other sports are certainly healthy and fun, but excessive competitiveness (especially in our sports-crazed culture) can quickly ruin a good game. I know of several high school athletes who quit the team not because they lacked sufficient skills, but because they were frustrated by an excessive emphasis on individual ability.

On the other side of the coin, organized sports – like the games of grade school and early childhood – can provide regular opportunities to bring boys and girls, young men and women together for a common purpose. There is nothing like healthy athletic competition to pull children out of themselves and inspire them to give their best. If parents and teachers guide games so that the players keep this in mind, even a highly competitive event can be a positive experience for everyone involved. That, after all, is the point of recreation.

CHAPTER TWENTY-TWO

Physical Work

WE LIVE IN AN ERA when modern technology has re-
lieved us of almost every task our grandparents once
performed – from chopping wood to carrying water. Technology is not the only reason for this, however: attitudes
to children and work have changed dramatically in the last
hundred years, and to many children physical work is
a wholly foreign idea. In many homes, parents simply
do not expect their children to work, even to make their
own beds, wash the dishes, or mow the lawn. A friend
recently wrote to me:

> I'm not sure my generation ever really grew up. We don't
> know what it is to make sacrifices, to give unselfishly in
> ways that won't ever be recognized. Many of us are still
> seeking the perfect partner, the perfect car, or some other
> kind of elusive happiness.

While no one in his right mind could desire a return to the

days of child labor, sometimes it seems that the pendulum has swung too far the other way, that we have forgotten the value of work as an important tool of education. Physical work will not harm children; in fact, it usually does wonders for them. When you give a child a chore to do, you develop his or her ability to follow instructions. In helping to see it through to completion, you help the child build initiative and perseverance. Afterwards, you can praise him or her and instill pride in a job well done.

Where I grew up – the hinterland of subtropical Paraguay – hard physical work was part of daily life. One did not need to look for it. There was no indoor plumbing, no central heating, and, for many years, no electricity. Meals were cooked on an open fire, and there was always wood to split and stack, and water to carry. Grass was cut with a machete; it was coarse, heavy, and high-growing, especially after rainfall. Often I used to grumble about the never-ending work, but my parents had no pity: "Good, hard work makes a man," they always said. In retrospect, I am grateful for every chore I did. I see now how work taught me self-discipline and concentration and prepared me for the responsibilities of fatherhood.

Like adults, children need the discipline of work. Without it, they quickly lose focus and direction and become easily distracted. All too often, physical inactivity and laziness is followed by inner lethargy and, after that, sin. Perhaps that is why Thoreau, a champion of the disciplined life, was fond of saying, "If you would avoid uncleanness and all the sins, work earnestly, though it be at cleaning a stable."[34]

Finding meaningful work for older children and young adults today requires more inventiveness than it did a generation ago. After all, it doesn't take much regular physical labor to maintain a house in the city, or even a suburban yard. Yet it is worth the effort. Without work, children are denied the benefit of learning to carry responsibility, even if only in the form of a small daily chore around the house.

If we can help our children see work in the sense of service to others, every task they do can be given meaning, whether it is a matter of mundane chores around the home, an after-school job, menial work, or "real" work in an internship or training program.

Learning to work hard means far more than learning to sweat: it means building character. Our children need to grow up loving work, not avoiding it. Let us teach them to find inspiration in the face of challenges and difficulties, not frustration. And let us instill in them the desire to carry out everything they do with joy.

CHAPTER TWENTY-THREE

Family Interaction

OVER THE LAST THREE DECADES, study after study has shown that family life has a greater influence over a child's mental development and academic performance than anything else, even school. Without parental interaction, it seems, effective education remains an elusive goal. To most readers this should come as no surprise; after all, anyone who has been around children knows that they thrive on parental love and attention.

I have emphasized throughout this book that anything a family can do *together* is worthwhile. Regular family meals are especially important. Research even shows a correlation between test scores and the frequency of meals taken together by the family. Eating together gives parents and children an excellent opportunity to talk about many things – school activities, plans for the weekend, or ideas for the next family trip. Mealtimes can also provide occasion for broadening a child's horizons through discussions about local and world news, current events and issues, and books they are reading at home or at school. Encourage your children to contribute their perspectives to the conversation.

Don't forget the significance of breakfast. When my six sisters and I were growing up, our parents used to eat breakfast with us every school day and then send us off with an encouraging word. They did this for years, until my youngest sister graduated from high school. Aside from providing a reason to get together on a regular basis, this beginning to the day often made all the difference at school.

If you have school age children, welcome them home when they return in the afternoon. Take time to talk to them about their day. Just as important, listen to them and show a genuine interest in everything they have to tell you. When they bring home assignments, make sure they do them, and do them neatly. Most children find ways to get out of doing their homework whenever they can, but if you insist that they see it through (setting a regular time and place will help) they will soon become used to making it a regular part of their afternoon or evening.

Help your children with their homework – they will be unendingly grateful to you. Children are surprisingly responsive to adult enthusiasm for their work, and often it won't take much to turn drudgery into something they look forward to doing well. Even if you lack the background in a subject like math, where teaching methods have changed drastically, you can still show interest in your child's progress.

When a child has difficulty in a particular subject, find ways to build his or her confidence by providing extra encouragement, especially if he or she has low self-esteem. Keep in close touch with teachers too. If the problem persists and seems unsolvable, inquire about tutoring or even remedial help. Remember, however, that a child's academic progress is a reflection of only one part of his or her life. Don't make too much of it, and don't compare him or her with other children. A child who shows consistent effort and self-discipline deserves as much praise as one who sails through every course with flying colors, even if his or her report card is not as good. I used to spend hours and hours on my homework, but I still got C's and D's. I failed several subjects. Yet instead of scolding me, my parents always encouraged me, and this kept me going.

Parents who neglect to take an active interest in their children because they are "too busy" do them an injustice. Children long for contact with their parents. Most will not be able to verbalize this longing, perhaps, and some may not even be conscious of it, but it is there in every child. As parents, we must always be ready to answer it.

CHAPTER TWENTY-FOUR

The Importance
of Reading

IF YOU LOVE YOUR CHILDREN, read to them. There is no
better way to spend time with them. Whether fiction, bi-
ography, history, fairy tales, or stories from the Bible, anything you choose can bring you together in a way that will
have a positive impact on your relationship for the rest of
their lives.

It is never too early to read to a child. Even a baby enjoys
the sound of his or her mother's or father's voice and the vi-
sual stimulation of a simple fold-out book. And an older
infant or toddler, although unable to sit for a proper story,
loves to flip through a picture book or colorful magazine.
Reading to children is the first, most vital step in preparing
them to read on their own: it develops their ability to sit still
and concentrate, even if for a short time.

Albert Einstein said, "If you want your children to be
brilliant, tell them fairy tales." Legends, tales, and folklore

in general provide wonderful material for a child's imagination. Beyond that, they contain themes of great inner value: suffering and redemption, the victory of good over evil, the mastery of fear, the spirit of adventure, and the importance of a virtuous life – of humility, purity, generosity, and self-sacrifice. Of course, not only fairy tales, but all good stories, and in a special way the wonderful, simple stories of the Old and New Testaments, can help children to make sense of their lives and to affirm their childlike recognition of truth.

Reading and being read to are vital activities: they spark the desire to learn. If this desire is missing, no amount of parental effort will help. Once your children can read by themselves, continue to read to them, but encourage them to read on their own too. Suggest good books – books that will inspire them to pick up others – and tell them which ones you loved as a child. If their interests are different than your own, ask yourself what might inspire them. What are your children's hobbies and favorite classes? If they don't seem to have any real hobbies or guiding interests, think of topics that might stimulate them to pick one up, and help them find books on the topic.

If a child has difficulty learning to read or seems to have no interest in reading, read to him or her all the more. In this way he or she will be able to keep abreast of peers who gain additional knowledge by reading on their own.

Reading to your children at home can break down the boundaries they may perceive between home and school. It sends them the message that learning is not only valuable, but fun. Every minute spent around a story can further cement the bond between you and your children at a crucial age and give them something they will treasure for the rest of their lives.

CHAPTER TWENTY-FIVE

Academics

IN MANY SCHOOL DISTRICTS across the nation, the curriculum has become increasingly geared to the production of academic "superkids." The stated intention is to prepare children to meet the challenges of the 21st century, and that in itself may be commendable, but the means by which this goal is achieved is worrying.

Many educators and public policy experts press for higher academic standards because they are worried that the United States is losing its competitive edge in the international market. Their fear is valid enough. Already for years, the test scores of American students have lagged far behind those of students from other industrialized nations. Yet is the root of the problem really a matter of academics?

Many of today's children deal daily with issues almost unheard of in their grandparents' (or even parents') day – from teen pregnancy and the accompanying fear of AIDS, to guns in the playground, widespread domestic violence, and homelessness. (Even in our suburban New York county, an estimated 400 students live in shelters for the homeless.) Is it really any surprise that SAT scores and literacy levels are down, that geographical knowledge is at an all-time low, that math and science performance continues to drop off? Isn't it simplistic to think that change can be brought about merely by lengthening the school day or adding Saturday sessions?

It is well known that even as performance levels continue to drop, increasing numbers of high school and grade school children are being driven into depression – and in some cases, suicide – by pressures they are not equipped to cope with. Granted, academic work should and must be done. Children should be expected to work hard, to be stretched and intellectually stimulated. They must be taught to articulate their feelings, to write, to read, to develop and defend an idea; to think critically. But just as important, we must instill in them such basic values as honesty, humility, open-mindedness, and compassion and, as Jonathan Kozol puts it, "invest in their gentle hearts as well as their competitive skills."[35]

Yet before we preach about virtues to our children, we must ask ourselves whether we really model these virtues in our own lives. Are we truly friends, guardians, and parents to our children when they need us? Are our homes places where they feel welcome, wanted, and loved, places where they feel secure and safe? Do we show them, by the way we treat them, that we feel their lives count?

It is no small challenge to encourage children to do their best in a way that affirms their God-given abilities, to take into account the circumstances each of them comes from, and to stretch them without subjecting them to undue pressure. Every child is different. Some are brilliant; some are capable but lazy; others are poorly equipped intellectually but amazingly gifted with their hands. One is an only child; another comes last in a large family. Still another is a child of immigrants. If we truly love our children, we will not see these differences as problems, but welcome them and allow them to enrich us. Further, we will place equal value on every ability, whether practical or academic, and encourage each child to reach his or her full potential in every area.

We must dispel from the very start the illusion that some occupations are more important than others, and point out to our children that the world needs plumbers, carpenters, and farmers just as much as it needs lawyers, doctors, teachers, and musicians. It would be foolish to pretend otherwise, especially in a society like ours, where a one-sided emphasis on academics has led to a glut of white-collar professionals who look for meaningful work in vain.

The situation in many schools in Japan, where academic excellence is prized above all else, is certainly more extreme than in the United States, but it indicates the pitfalls of an educational philosophy that assesses children's worth wholly in terms of their achievement in the classroom. According to a recent article in *The New York Times:*

These days, to be a tiny tot in many Japanese families is not to play leisurely on swings and seesaws, but to spend hours at desks in classrooms memorizing stories, learning homonyms, making calendars, putting colored chips in sequences, taking achievement tests, and walking on balance beams – all before the child is four.[36]

The writer goes on to say that many parents rush their two- and three-year-olds into "cram schools" so that they can pass the entrance exams into the best kindergartens. Without admission into these, there is little chance for admission into the best elementary schools, the best high schools, and so on. "Many parents are deeply troubled by…the examination hell; but if they try to spare their sons and daughters the ordeal…they may be sentencing them to second-rate futures."

Clearly, the root of the problem described above is a deeply spiritual one. It betrays a view of children that values them in terms of what we, their parents and educators, would like them to become, and rates them according to their success in a future that we have defined for them. It leaves them little or no room to be children.

How different our approach could be if we recognized that *every child* is a thought of God! Then we would see that the education of each child must be God-inspired, and that in every case it must be undertaken with the goal of unfolding what God has already placed within the child. Most important, we would begin to understand what Jesus really meant when he said, "You must become like children."

CHAPTER TWENTY-SIX

The Gifted Child

SOMETIMES IT SEEMS that certain children get all the lucky breaks, while others have a rough time simply coping with life. One child consistently brings home straight A's on her report card and goes on to become the valedictorian of her graduating class, another cooks with flair, and another has musical talent or athletic ability. Still another seems gifted in every way, with a handsome build, lots of friends, good grades on every report card, and the best throwing arm in the school. Then there is the child who struggles and slogs through his homework every night but never gets a good grade, the girl who feels she is all arms and legs, or the boy who's always getting into trouble. Obviously, every child – every human being – is blessed with different gifts and abilities, strengths and weaknesses. Children must be brought up to accept this fact. But parents must accept it themselves and refrain from comparing their children with others or pushing them to be people that God may not have intended them to be.

In my experience as a father and grandfather, a gifted child has a special burden to carry. It is the same with physical beauty, which has been called the "golden curse." Too often parents tend to show off a beautiful or talented child, flatter her, or treat her with favoritism. Teachers are prone to doing the same. If only they realized what harm they are doing to the soul of the child! Not only do children who are made overly conscious of their talents or abilities have difficulty relating to their peers; often, they grow up forgetting that their gifts are not their own, but given to them by God to be used for his glory. Sometimes they even think that they are inherently better than others, and feel that they have more to contribute to the world than their peers. If a sibling or friend of such a child happens to be a slow learner, or is even just somewhat less brilliant or assertive, it may take only one slightly negative remark to heighten his awareness of his own lack of gifts in a damaging way.

It is never helpful to label a child in a way that assesses his competitive value, either as a superstar or an underachiever. God has a purpose and a plan for every one, and to ignore this fact is unhealthy. Parents and teachers should do all they can to encourage and develop a child's gifts and abilities, but they should never do it through flattery, and certainly never at the expense of another child whose gifts are different.

Given the highly competitive climate of today's world, especially the shrinking job market, it is understandable that our educational system puts greater and greater emphasis on preparing children for the fast track. All the same, we dare not forget that to idolize a child's gifts, no matter what they are, is to do him or her a grave disservice. The world may well need Albert Einsteins and Isaac Newtons, but it also needs men and women who relate to each other on the simple, down-to-earth matters of the heart that give life its deepest meaning. It needs people like Paul, who recognized: "If I understand all mysteries and all knowledge but have not love, I am nothing" (1 Cor. 13:2).

I still remember my parents' insistence that no matter what we children did later in life, we should never let pride in our gifts prevent us from humbly serving others. When my younger sister Monika was still at medical school, they wrote to her that even if she became a doctor she should never despise a life of serving, of washing the feet of her brothers and sisters, as it were, like Jesus washed his disciples' feet.

Sometimes common sense and practical know how are more useful than intellectual ability. The child who has the hardest time learning to read and do long division, for example, may be the only one in the family who is able to repair the lawnmower or to take an engine apart. One summer a teenager I knew, a young man who had the highest IQ ever recorded by the local school system, repainted a neighbor's roof. He climbed up with his paint bucket and roller and started to paint – from the bottom to the top. When he got to the top he realized he was in trouble. On the way down, he slipped on the fresh paint, fell off the roof, and broke his leg. It was a painful lesson, but a valuable one.

No one is too gifted, or too poor in gifts, to love. Whether brilliant or dull, disabled or athletic, all of us can give our lives in service to others, and to Christ. His way, the way of compassion and humility, should be the moral compass for each of us and for our children.

CHAPTER TWENTY-SEVEN

Teaching Science

THE ROOT OF THE WORD "science" is "to know," and its original meaning is simply the possession of knowledge as opposed to ignorance or misunderstanding. God gave us our brains and the ability to discover, to observe, and to learn. For us who believe, what we learn gives us reason for praise; it fills us with wonder at the omnipotence of the Creator and the beauty of everything he has made – from the sky at morning to the buds of spring.

In the same way that we can see the hand of God in the world around us, we can recognize it in the branches of science that analyze it: biology, chemistry, physics, astronomy, and mathematics. Far from weakening our faith, these can strengthen our awe at the power of God manifested in creation and strengthen our love for him.

Unfortunately, much of what is taught today in the name of science is characterized by a complete disregard for God. Naturalism – the belief that the physical or material world is all that exists – is treated as a basic fact, and anything that questions its assumptions is quickly dismissed as religious superstition. William Provine, a biology professor at Cornell, writes:

> Modern science directly implies that the world is organized strictly in accordance with mechanistic principles. There is no purposive principle whatsoever in nature. There are no gods and no designing forces that are rationally detectable...
>
> Second, modern science directly implies that there are no inherent moral or ethical laws, no absolute guiding principles for human society.
>
> Third...the individual human becomes an ethical person by means of two primary mechanisms: heredity and environmental influences. That is all there is.
>
> Fourth, we must conclude that when we die, we die and that is the end of us...
>
> Finally, free will as it is traditionally conceived...simply does not exist. [37]

In general, any discussion of science will sooner or later bump on one of the many basic disagreements between such attitudes and the attitude of faith held by most believers. Nowhere, however, are the lines as sharply drawn as in the debate over the origin of life. I myself wholeheartedly believe with the apostle John that "in the beginning was the Word" and that "through him everything was made." At the same time, I cannot agree with the self-righteous scorn heaped on all aspects of evolutionary theory by many fundamentalists, especially the many so-called creationists who insist on interpreting the seven days described in Genesis as literal twenty-four-hour days.

What route can an educator (or parent) who is leery of both viewpoints take? To begin with, let me say that I see no purpose in giving equal space to every theory and hoping that one's children will find their own way. Why hinder their childlike faith by confusing them with materialistic theories that deny the existence of the Spirit? Even though the story of Genesis may prove nothing (as Hebrews 11:3 says, "By faith alone we perceive that the whole universe was fashioned by the Word of God, so that the visible came forth from the invisible"), anyone who is honest with himself must agree that there are no scientific proofs for contrary explanations either. Conflicting theories abound, and opinions are set against opinions. New "proofs" are given recognition in the headlines one week but disappear the next as others emerge. In one journal we read about the discovery of yet another previously missing link; in another we find that new advances in molecular biology place evolutionary theory under greater attack than ever before. In the end, we are still left with more questions than answers, with more wonder than actual knowledge. Even the greatest scientists of this century recognized that. Einstein himself is said to have commented that anyone who is "not lost in rapturous awe of the power and glory of the Mind behind the universe is as good as a burnt-out candle."

Admittedly, the Bible leaves the inquiring mind with more than a few questions. In Genesis we read that God created the world and everything in it in six days, and that on the seventh day he rested. We read, too, that he created man on the sixth day, and made him of clay. Then in 2 Peter 3:8 we read that "for God one day is like a thousand years." Whether the sixth day was twenty-four hours or one thousand years, or whether the piece of clay had for a time the form and stance of an ape, is not at all important. For the believer, the decisive issue is the fact that at a certain moment God breathed his breath – the breath of life – into man, and in this way made him in his image. At that inconceivably great moment, man became a living creature endowed with an eternal soul.

Whether "creationism" or "evolutionism" carries the day need not detract from our faith in the Creator of all things. In the end, the essential conflict is not so much *how* human beings came about, but *what* they are in relation to the rest of life. Even if it were proved that we humans evolved from ape-like creatures, I would still believe we are set apart; that we are not just one species among the many that inhabit our earth, but exist on a higher plane. As human beings, we possess consciences to know right from wrong; hearts that can feel love and compassion, and minds able to acquire and develop abstract knowledge. Because of this, we are responsible for our thoughts and actions and must answer to God for the choices we make.

Whatever we teach our children about the creation of the world and the origin of man (or about any other topic of science, for that matter), let us remind them – and ourselves – that at root, the controversy lies in the eternal conflict between God and human pride. Perhaps that is the most vital recognition we can pass on to them. Naturally, we ourselves must recognize this first. Eberhard Arnold writes, "[As an educator] you must learn wonder. In the knowledge of your own smallness, marvel at the greatness of the divine mystery that lies hidden in all things and behind all things…Only those who look with the eyes of children can lose themselves in the object of their wonder."[38]

Darwin and Huxley promoted evolution and scientific humanism as necessary counterbalances to the "error" of faith, and Nietzsche spoke of an *Übermensch* ("superman") who existed in God's place. We believe, on the other hand, that redemption will never come about through an evolutionary process or through our own human efforts, but through God's kingdom, which breaks in at his time and in his way, whenever men and women seek its spirit. Ultimately, that recognition is the basis of our thirst for knowledge and the goal of all our longings. For us, it is truth in its simplest and most powerful form.

CHAPTER TWENTY-EIGHT

Sex Education

SEX EDUCATION in the public schools began as an offshoot of the sexual revolution of the 1960s. Like the revolution itself, sex education as it is commonly taught in our schools is based on the premise (even if not stated) that sex is primarily a form of recreation. Its goal, therefore, is to instruct teens on how to engage in sexual activity while avoiding pitfalls such as unwanted pregnancies or sexually transmitted diseases. It is unlikely that this goal will be openly admitted, even by the strongest advocates of sex education. Yet an honest look at the materials used in most schools can only lead to the conclusion that this is indeed the actual intent.

Most sex education, it must be said, takes place not in the classroom but outside of it. The message of the sexual revolution – "if it feels good, do it" – is broadcast more boldly every year on television, in movies and videos, and in popular songs, books, and magazines. Even if sex education were completely removed from our schools, our children would still receive the same miseducation from the entertainment industry.

As parents, we must ask, "What have thirty years of sex education in the public schools, and thirty years of increasingly explicit sex in the media, brought to our society?" The answer is: disaster. Sexual activity has increased dramatically among teenagers and led to the highest rates of teen pregnancy, abortion, and venereal disease in the world. The incidence of AIDS is rising higher among teenagers than among any other group. Meanwhile, marriage has declined to such an extent that 30% of American children are born out of wedlock. Along with a divorce rate that has quadrupled, the result is that more and more children are being raised without a responsible father in the home. The erosion of family life has in turn contributed to many other social problems, from the decline of discipline in the public schools to a dramatic increase in violent teen crime (including rape), suicide, and general emotional disturbances.[39]

Of course none of these catastrophes can be blamed solely and directly on sex education in the schools, or even on the media. Both are effects, though certainly also contributing causes of a larger problem: our society's almost complete abandonment of the biblical understanding of human sexuality. Instead of being guided by a sense of reverence for the mystery of men and women as beings created in the image of God, public and private attitudes toward sex are driven by the view that sex is a mere animal appetite to be gratified by whatever means necessary.

Unfortunately, most of the answers proposed to solve all this – well-meaning as some of them may be – are short-sighted. Some people suggest ridding our schools of sex education classes entirely; others support boycotting agencies that produce sexually explicit advertising. Still others feel the answer lies in harshly penalizing young women who become pregnant, for example by cutting off welfare assistance to teen mothers. (This last "solution" is down-right cruel: it punishes women who have already been victimized by the irresponsible attitudes and sexual pressures of the rest of society, and in particular by the men who father their babies.)

Instead of putting our hopes in the manipulation of politics and social policy, or the reform of the welfare system, I strongly feel that we must take the responsibility upon ourselves as parents and create our own revolution by bringing the issues of sexuality to our children in a way that is both realistic and reverent. We must teach our children that sexual activity fulfills its divine purpose only in the context of a loving marriage, and we must approach sex itself in a way that connects the physical act to its spiritual significance, and the life of the body to the life of the soul.

I am aware that this is an unpopular view. People say that sex education in the home never works: parents won't bring up the subject, and children are left to inform themselves by alternative, usually less desirable, means. Judging by the number of sexually confused teens in the world today, many parents do fail miserably. Yet why should we admit defeat? It is high time that the trend was reversed, that parents shoulder their responsibilities again and become their children's primary educators, with the school providing secondary support – not vice versa.

Over the years I have counseled dozens of couples who felt uncomfortable or inadequate in speaking to their children about sex. I have always encouraged them to speak to their children anyway. There is no harm in asking the advice of a close friend, a pastor, or a trusted teacher. Yet parents should never forget that their children are first and foremost *theirs*. When parents relinquish to others such a centrally important aspect of their children's upbringing, they rob parenthood of one of its fundamental tasks and miss a vital opportunity to build openness and trust.

Because the right time to approach sex education will be different for each child, I hesitate to say when it should be done. I will say, however, that one should take every opportunity that comes to instill reverence, and answer a child's questions openly and without embarrassment, though without giving him or her more information than asked for.

In my experience it is wise not to give a child too much "scientific" information too soon. When a three-year-old wants to know where babies come from, it is enough to say that God gives babies to their parents as a special gift. This will satisfy the little questioner – and it is also deeply true. An older child will be able to understand that the new life comes into being through the uniting of a special cell from the father with a special cell from the mother.

When a child reaches puberty, it is time to explain sexual intercourse and its role as a means for a husband and wife to express their love to each other and bring new life into the world. Each couple will find their own way to talk about this. The indispensable key is that as parents, we ourselves have reverence for sex. If we view sex as a beautiful and holy gift from God, we will be able to convey this to our children.

Again, don't miss opportunities to teach your children! You were once a teenager yourself, and surely you had questions of your own as you grew up. Do your utmost to ensure that your children will be better equipped than you were to understand and handle their sexuality. The best way to help children feel secure about themselves is to give them a secure relationship with you. Let them know that you are there for them, ready to talk, and ready to listen.

Lastly, don't forget that actions speak louder than words. The way you and your spouse (and other adults) behave in front of your children is far more significant than what you tell them about the reproductive process. In short, remember that you shape your children's attitudes to sex long before you talk about it. Be an example to your children. That is always the best education.

Homosexuality

Although I have intentionally refrained from suggesting exactly what parents should teach their children about sex, I would like to say a few words about homosexuality. Aside from abortion, few other topics are as inflammatory, especially when it appears in a public school curriculum.

As most gay rights advocates will admit, their main goal in bringing homosexuality into the classroom is to legitimize their lifestyle by fostering understanding and acceptance. Citing separation of church and state, many of them promote the idea of a learning environment where no values are imposed on students. Increasingly, they succeed in pressuring school administrators and curriculum committees to avoid "religion-based" ideas such as abstinence and to support the promulgation of their own "neutral" agenda instead.

Few opponents dare to stick out their necks to point out that a neutral, value-free classroom simply cannot exist. Dress codes and campaigns for drug-free schools may indeed represent values (so do ideals like honesty in test-taking and courtesy to teachers), yet on the opposite side of the coin, so do sex education classes in which students are taught to reject the teachings of the Bible and to believe that homosexual activity is normal and acceptable.

Let us not be swayed in our faith by the current arguments that excuse every sin by explaining it away. Even if homosexual urges were proved to be "natural" – that is, caused by genetic factors – would that make them right? Don't both the Old and New Testaments make it clear that such desires are always sinful? Despite modern psychology's emphasis on analyzing man as an animal with animal-like urges, and its teaching that it is unhealthy to suppress these urges (and despite Freud's claim that sex is every person's prime motivating force) let us not forget that man was still created in the image of God. The attempt to explain any aspect of human life without God, who brought it into being, is a grave mistake.

We should never try to force our own values on others or treat them harshly because we disagree with them. We must bring up our children to be compassionate to every individual they meet. All the same, there is no reason why we should not speak out when we feel their moral education is at stake. We cannot stand silent simply because others regard our viewpoints as unenlightened or oppressive. If we take seriously Jesus' call to follow him, we will witness not only to his love, but also to the uncompromising clarity of his teachings.*

---

*For a more detailed discussion of homosexuality, see the author's book *A Plea for Purity: Sex, Marriage, and God.*

CHAPTER TWENTY-NINE

Art, Crafts, and Music

IN SPITE OF THE FACT that most school systems treat art as a sideline, more and more educators are coming to realize what the art teachers have been saying all along: art is not a frill, but one of the most important and enjoyable areas of a child's education. Art opens new doors of experience by helping children to see the world around them in new ways. It sharpens their powers of observation, heightens their sense of appreciation, and awakens them to the possibilities of their own hands, hearts, and minds.

Art can help children to develop socially and emotionally, too. When they are encouraged to give form to their ideas, they learn the value of self-expression. In discovering their ability to create, they become conscious of their imagination and their freedom to make choices. And in mixing colors or combining materials to make new ones, they can learn to think in terms of change.

As a means to explore shapes and textures, quantities, sizes, and proportions, art can also aid children's intellectual development. It helps them to grasp the concepts they will need in learning to read, write, add, and subtract; it stimulates inquisitiveness, critical thinking, and a healthy self-confidence. Physically, it develops fine motor control and hand/eye coordination. In short, art is a window to new horizons in every sphere of life.

Small children need and love daily chances to experiment and explore, to "mess around" at their own unhurried pace. Let them crumple and tear magazines or newspapers, cut and paste scraps, shape playdough or clay. Let them scribble to their heart's content: it is as natural and necessary a step toward drawing and writing as crawling is to walking. Don't feel you have to be an artist yourself, and don't try to "teach" your child art. Help him (or her) to discover it for himself. The fact that blue and yellow make green means more to a child when he finds it out on his own.

Creativity should be encouraged from early on. In our Bruderhof schools our teachers have noted that if art is neglected in the lower grades when children are relatively uninhibited and free – willing to experiment, to make mistakes, and to try again – it will be more frustrating for them to try to express themselves when they are older.

In the first three or four years, the enormous joy and satisfaction a child experiences in the act of creation itself is the most important factor. Don't underestimate this. You may see the result of a project as its most significant aspect, but for the child, the value of the activity is not measured by the finished product. The fun of doing it is just as satisfying. Later, of course, the end result will become more and more important, and with it, the encouragement (and, when called for, constructive criticism) that lets the child know his or her art is valuable.

Always treat a child's work with respect. Never belittle it or criticize it. When children are made to feel that what they make is not only a form of self-expression but a gift to be shared, their enthusiasm for further progress will grow. Show appreciation by making suggestions: "Next week is Grandma's birthday. Why don't you give her that picture you painted?" A child's artwork has brightened the day of many a hospitalized friend, elderly neighbor, or local prison inmate.

Children are always eager to participate in life as fully as possible, and as parents and educators, we must continually find ways to respond to their eagerness. If we do not occupy them in constructive ways, we should not be surprised if they become restless and bored. With younger children the problem is easily solvable; with older ones, it can be more difficult. Kathy Mow, a Bruderhof artist who has taught in our schools for some forty years, writes:

As children, especially teenagers, grow up into young men and women, we must find ways to give them continual outlets for their creative urges. It is not fair to offer them a diet of passive activities only. Street graffiti, unusual hair-styles, or provocative dress, excessive peer-group identification – all these reflect the unfulfilled need for constructive self-expression.

The creative potential is there in each child, waiting to be developed. Aside from providing a way to spend many hours constructively, whether alone or with others, enjoyment in a particular craft or art form – painting, weaving, knitting, pottery, calligraphy, wood or metal work, building models – may grow into a hobby and, in some cases, into a guiding interest that helps a child to find a vocation later in life.

Music

Though many people tend to classify themselves and their children as "unmusical," music can speak to every heart and enrich every life. In a sense, it is a universal language that, according to the great Japanese teacher Shinichi Suzuki, lies hidden in every child. In some it may be apparent already in the cradle, and in others it may show itself only in adulthood; yet it is there. Whether a child grows up to be "musical" has perhaps less to do with inborn talent than with the time and care taken to develop and nourish him or her.

Music education in the first years should be approached as naturally as possible – simply as a means of providing stimulation through beauty. The issue at stake here goes beyond music; to quote Suzuki, it is a matter of nurturing children with love…"Children in their simplicity seek what is true, good, and beautiful…based on love."[40]

When words fail, music often seems to come closest in giving voice to what one feels within. At our Bruderhof communities, music has always played a significant role in this way: not as a discipline, nor as performance art, but as an expression of a shared experience. With a song for every mood and every occasion – Christmas, Easter, the birth of a baby, a wedding, the turning of the leaves, the return of summer – music can enrich life by bringing people together for celebrations or times of grief and adds meaning to even the most mundane event.

As children grow, the best way to build their appreciation for music is to sing together. An evening around the fire with a guitar or an hour spent singing around the piano may seem romantic or outdated to some, but there are few activities that bring a family together so closely. Even if both parents are unpracticed or lack musical gifts, a little enthusiasm can go a long way. Marlys Swinger, a Bruderhof composer and music teacher, writes:

> The language of music is a stepping stone to the soul of a child…It can be as natural as the beginning of speech. I have known children who hummed or chanted recognizable tunes before they said words! When parents encourage a child's musical development by singing to him and with him, it will only be a matter of months before the child knows dozens of songs.

The overall environment a child grows up in has as much to do with his development as with the particular music he is exposed to. Is the home a place of harmony and love, or one of discord? Has the child grown up with lullabies on his mother's lap, or does the only music in the house come from a radio on the kitchen table?

When your children are old enough to learn to read music, encourage them to join a school or church choir. If possible, inspire them to learn an instrument: aside from developing children musically, lessons encourage creative self-expression, concentration, and perseverance. Expose them to a variety of musical forms by taking them to concerts, and talk about the program afterward. What did the music say or mean? Was it good music? What constitutes "good" music?

In trying to decide whether or not your child should have music lessons, it is vital to consider the following: does the child really want lessons on the instrument? Is she ready to take on the discipline of daily practicing? Does she (and do her parents) realize that musical skills take years to acquire, that there is no quick magic? Often a child has no great ambitions – simply the desire to play the guitar so as to accompany her friends. In other instances a child will show unusual drive and practice for hours on her own initiative.

In order to give each child the chance at least to try his or her wings, we encourage all children in our schools to learn the recorder in the third grade. By this means, each of them is given a foundation in musical basics on a simple, inexpensive instrument and has the means for moving on, if he or she wishes, to another instrument.

Perhaps the best way to instill a love of music in children is to encourage them to join a choir, whether at school or church. Regardless of his or her ability, every child can benefit from the discipline and teamwork required in preparing a piece and, even more important, from the satisfaction of sharing the final performance with an audience. The great violinist Yehudi Menuhin writes:

> I can only think of music as something in every human being – a birthright. Music coordinates mind, body, and spirit. That doesn't mean each person must have a violin or piano: the greatest service to society would be if every school day began with singing. If people sing or play together, they have a feeling of individual coordination as well as coordination within the body of the group. I have never met a member of a choir who was depressed.[41]

CHAPTER THIRTY

Children and Nature

F RIEDRICH FROEBEL WRITES that if we are to fully reach our destiny – to reach it as whole beings – we must become unbroken units: we must "feel ourselves to be one not only with God and humanity, but also with nature."[42] In a sense, it is more a matter of returning to God and nature than becoming one with them. After all, each of us comes from the same source.

Children have an innate sense of wonder. They are clear-eyed, excited by everything they see: a worm in a puddle, a spider on the sidewalk, a family of ducklings in the park, frost patterns on a windowpane. We adults, on the other hand, tend to miss most of these things. We are more fascinated by the headlines than by a rainbow. Even if we try to take an interest in the world around us, the pace of our lives often prevents us from doing this in more than a superficial way. In addition, many of us do not live in God's world at all, but in a sterile environment of concrete and glass, carpeting and plastic, conditioned air, soft lights, and artificial plants. The same is true for greater and greater numbers of children, especially in large cities. We have become alienated from nature, and alienated from God.

How can we rediscover a genuine appreciation for the world around us? How can we preserve our children's sense of wonder, and how can we recapture it ourselves? In our Bruderhof schools we have found over many years that if we do not want our children to lose their closeness to God's world, we cannot simply teach them *about* it; we must bring them up *in* it. Our classrooms are empty as often as they are full, even on "regular" school days. We feel that growing and harvesting tomatoes in the school garden plot, measuring rainfall, pressing flowers or ferns, and watching birds are every bit as vital to our children's education as reading, writing, and arithmetic. Needless to say, even these can be learned by activities outdoors. One of the highlights of our school year each spring is maple sapping – an excellent way to combine math, science, nature study, and good hard work.

Bringing up children in nature is not just a matter of teaching them facts about the world around them. It means instilling in them the desire to learn. In many instances it is they who pave the way for us. Through their curiosity and eagerness we rediscover the marvels of the creation and feel a new reverence for all of life. How can one watch with a child as a butterfly emerges from a chrysalis, and not sense a miracle? How can one watch a mother robin feed its young, or watch puppies play, and not feel joy? How can one experience the changing of the seasons and not sense the rhythm and harmony of the universe?

Children who grow up in nature will not easily lose their sense of wonder; on the contrary, it will remain with them into adulthood. Sometimes it can even guide them in their search for faith. A former student in one of our schools, now a mother of four, recently wrote to me:

> In my teenage years and even earlier, a quiet walk in the woods or a few minutes watching the sun set were deep experiences for me – a healing during troubled times, a chance to find inner quiet, a physical way to come close to the creator. Being alone in nature, I found out how real God is.

Naturalist Rachel Carson writes in the same vein:

> What is the value of preserving and strengthening this sense of awe and wonder, this recognition of something beyond the boundaries of human existence? Is the exploration of the natural world just a pleasant way to pass the golden hours of childhood, or is there something deeper?
>
> I am sure there is something much deeper, something lasting and significant. Those who dwell, as scientists or laymen, among the beauties and mysteries of the earth, are never alone or weary of life. Whatever the vexations or concerns of their personal lives, their thoughts can find paths that lead to inner contentment and to renewed excitement in living. Those who contemplate the beauty of the earth find reserves of strength that will endure as long as life lasts. There is symbolic as well as actual beauty in

the migration of birds, the ebb and flow of the tides, the folded bud ready for the spring. There is something infinitely healing in the repeated refrains of nature – the assurance that dawn comes after the night, and spring after the winter.[43]

ANIMALS AND PETS

One of the simplest and most direct ways of bringing nature to children is exposing them to animals. In my childhood, in South America, animals played an all-important role: dogs and horses, monkeys, parrots, and other animals and birds were always around. Horses and oxen were the only means of transportation. My friends and I used to spend hours and hours on horseback, chasing ostriches, racing our horses, or simply exploring the wide expanses of the grassland. Our dogs followed us wherever we went. Looking back, I realize that these were unusually ideal conditions to grow up in, yet the point remains: no matter the circumstances, there are few things that bring children as much happiness as time spent with animals.

If you live in a rural area, finding animals will usually not be hard; if you live in a city or suburban area, the opportunities may be few and far between. All the same, it is worth the effort. Take time to go to a park or to the zoo, plan a weekend trip into the country, or visit a dairy or horse farm and ask the owner if you can see the animals. You will be surprised how little it takes to give your children something they can treasure as a memory for the rest of their lives.

Even better, buy a pet. When you give children an animal to care for, you give them a responsibility. Teach them to look after the little creature just like they look after themselves: "You've had your breakfast; now it's your rabbit's turn." Or, "It's Saturday – time to clean the hamster's cage." Sometimes a pet can even be a help in drawing children out of themselves, particularly in the case of an only child or one who has few or no close friends.

Caring for pets can also teach a child many things about the cycle of life. The death of a much-loved dog, hamster, or hen is an important event in a child's life and should not be brushed off lightly. It is an important moment to talk about death. In the same way, watching a mother rabbit create a nest and prepare to give birth can provide a springboard for valuable discussions about reproduction and birth.

Most important, taking care of a pet encourages compassion. Every child is attracted to a running spider or a jumping toad, and many will gleefully go after it. Older children, especially, may throw sticks or stones at a bird or animal, or try to step on a beetle or lizard. Though most will respond to a gentle admonition, some will not. For children who persist, learning to look after a pet can help them to overcome their childish tendency to cruelty and instill in them reverence for life.

CHAPTER THIRTY-ONE

Home Schooling

HOME SCHOOLING in the United States is no longer an insignificant or unorganized movement. Although almost nonexistent twenty years ago, it continues to spread rapidly. In the early 1980s there were 15,000 home schoolers; since then the number has escalated to about 1.5 million.[44] Home schoolers have not only become better networked, but are accomplishing many good results.

It is no accident that more and more people are educating their children at home. Despite the many dedicated individuals who teach in public schools or who care for children, today's schools and day care centers are in serious trouble. Fewer and fewer children are receiving the nurture, attention, values, and skills they need in order to flourish. Tied together with this is the fact that many children today spend very little quality time with their parents. Family life is fast becoming extinct. Home schooling is an attempt to return the family to children – children who desperately long for the loving authority that only parents can give.

There are many good reasons why parents home-school their children. Some couples feel that by giving their children one-on-one attention they are able to give them a better, more rounded education. Many home-school for religious and moral reasons. Learning from Mom or Dad can secure the child with an atmosphere of faith and a moral environment that fosters character and discipline.

Some couples home-school simply to solidify their own sense of family togetherness. Still others are concerned about the physical safety of their sons and daughters in increasingly violent school settings. These reasons – and there are surely many others – are both understandable and justified.

In recent months I have read many articles on home schooling, and the more I have read, the more enthusiastic I have become. One thing is clear: as churches, we need to give more credit to the parents who make up this movement. Despite its growing pains, it is providing an answer for growing numbers of children whose educational needs were not being met. Perhaps most significantly, it has encouraged new dialogue about the importance of better communication between the various sectors of the educational community – private, public, and parochial – and the home.

Obviously this book is not the place for an in-depth study of home schooling. In any case, the issue at stake is not whether one set of principles is better than another, but whether each child's eductional needs are being adequately met.

All the same, I want to make several short, personal observations. First, although an increasing number of fathers are becoming involved with their children's education at home, it is good to remember that in most cases, the burden of home schooling still falls largely on the mother, who is often the one who also cleans, cooks, shops, washes the laundry, and takes care of any children still in the home. Women who home-school their children in addition to doing all this deserve praise for their willingness to take on such a burden for their convictions, and they should expect the full support of their husbands.

Second, most parents do not have the resources to teach their children beyond the elementary level, and sooner or later integration into a public or private school system may become unavoidable. At the Bruderhof, where we have integrated many home-schooled children into our private schools over the years, we have found that the step is not an easy one. Often these children lagged behind the others of their class academically; in some cases the gap was two years or more. Such a gap is difficult to breach. For one thing, there is material that the new child needs to catch up on in addition to current assignments; then, too, the child, who is suddenly conscious that he is behind his peers, needs extra encouragement, attention, and help.

Admittedly, many home-schooled students who are integrated into public systems come out ahead of their peers academically. Yet even then, social adjustment problems may remain, especially when the home-schooled child has been brought up in an overly sheltered environment, or when a parent has been the sole caregiver, teacher, friend, and playmate. Home schoolers are becoming increasingly aware of this danger and are concentrating their efforts on building mutual support systems with other families; they are also providing social environments beyond the home for their children. This is commendable, but also vital: parents and children need more than each other to flourish. God has created us for community with others.

What is the best route for parents who question the wisdom of sending their children to public school but cannot afford a private one? Obviously, there is no single answer; every couple, every child, every school district is different. Yet I am certain that no matter the setting – the home, private school, parochial school, or public school – ways can be found for parents to raise their children according to their own values. Even in cases where a couple is forced by circumstances to enroll their children in a public school they would rather avoid, they do not have to give their children's spiritual education up for lost.

In our communities, the lack of sufficiently trained personnel makes public high school the only real option (we run our own schools from K-8), yet we have always found that if we are willing to do our part, the school will do theirs. Every school has at least a handful of teachers who are genuinely concerned for the moral education of the children in their care, and most will be happy to talk over parents' concerns regarding classroom discussions, texts, or audio-visual materials. More often than not, relationships with faculty and staff must be initiated by parents, yet it is rewarding to see how regular contact, whether by phone or in person, can build lasting friendships with teachers and administrators.

Most important (as I have emphasized earlier in this book), there must be a relationship of mutual trust between parents and children. Without it, even the most guarded home-school setting will guarantee nothing; but with it, the worst experiences of the school day can become opportunities for exchange.

When children feel genuine interest and trust on the part of their parents, they will be willing to discuss openly everything they experience at school. Further, they will not resent their parents' guidance and correction, because they will feel it is administered for their own good. Finally, they will dare to take a firm stand against whatever negative peer pressure they might meet during the school day and develop enough strength of character to withstand any ridicule they may have to put up with as a consequence. Even if painful, this is always a valuable lesson.

CHAPTER THIRTY-TWO

The Transition to Adulthood

I T IS A PRIVILEGE to be with young adults; to work with them, to share their joys and struggles, to be a friend to them, and to guide them toward God as they enter adulthood. Granted, adolescence is not a smooth phase of life, and there are very few teenagers who pass through it without at least a few rough patches. For many, it is the most turbulent time of their lives.

Everyone knows that teens' bodies and minds develop and change tremendously during adolescence, yet we sometimes forget that this causes their whole outlook to change too. Suddenly they have left childhood behind and entered the adult world, and even though most of them may be relatively uncertain of their goals in life, they are determined to spread their wings and try out their new freedoms. On top of this they are faced at almost every turn with the unavoidable tension between submitting to peer pressure on the one hand and parental authority on the other.

Adolescence can be perplexing to fathers and mothers too. Try as they might to help their children enter adulthood without losing the values they have struggled to instill in them, it often seems that everything is set against them. Most teens spend precious little time with their parents, and in a very real sense "parenting" falls to high school teachers, classmates and friends, and the ever present media.

Having said all this, I still firmly believe that adolescence can be a wonderful time, especially in the sense of providing parents with the last opportunities to cement family bonds before their children leave home and go their separate ways in the adult world. It may be a difficult period of life, but why should it be a particularly negative one? Is it possible that psychologists and sociologists have overemphasized the downside of adolescence to such an extent in the last forty years that our children cannot help living out the stereotypical adult fears?

I have seen time and again that if parents build a foundation of love and trust when their children are small, it is possible to guide them through their teen years without locking horns at every step. Naturally, all children go through a rebellious stage at one time or another; and the older they are at the point they rebel, the more effort it will take to come through. All the same, we should never forget the ups and downs of our own teen years. Why should we hold our children to a higher standard? Let us always seek to have patience and love in our dealings with them, even when we are tempted to throw them out of the house. Let us be friends as well as parents to them.

Jesus stresses the importance of daily forgiveness, and this is especially vital in relationships with teenagers. Even if they test us to the limit – even if they break every rule – they should never have to live in fear of losing our love. Teens do need to learn to take the consequences when they have done wrong, but they must also realize that we will always love them no matter what they do. If we are not able to forgive them fully when they admit their mistakes, they will lose their trust in us. Johann Christoph Blumhardt writes:

> Often parents demand too much submission from adolescent or grown-up children; they put a certain pressure on them even in trifling matters, as if they were still small children. They are intolerant toward them…These parents correct, punish, and find fault far too much, and there is never an atmosphere of friendliness.[45]

In my experience, the root of the problem Blumhardt describes is often a false understanding of love. In a family held together by an unhealthy emotionalism, parents tend to "love" their children by hanging on to them in a possessive, overprotective way. They pamper them and hope to be loved in return for their attention, and when they receive only resentment instead, they are hurt and angry. Not surprisingly, the results are disastrous. When parents take time to listen to a child, they will find that there is often a justified reason for his or her rebellion – at the very least, a fragment of truth in what he or she is trying to say.

If we truly love our children, we will not put pressure on them, make claims on them, or try to plan their future according to our wishes, but allow them the freedom to become whatever God intends them to become. When they lack direction, we may have to channel their energies toward a positive end; when they seem confused or insecure, we will need to offer them extra guidance and support. On the whole, however, we will see them as gifts from God and look at ourselves as their guardians, not their owners or masters.

Sometimes the most critical experience of the transition to adulthood is the way a young man or woman leaves his or her parents' home. Whether moving out in order to attend school, to start a job, or to set up a separate apartment, the manner in which parents and child part ways can profoundly influence their relationship for many years.

In cases where a child has been brought up with an attitude of respect and accountability to others, difficult decisions such as where to go to school and how to pay for it can be worked out easily enough. In families where children are used to considering nothing but their own wishes and "rights," however, the transition may be extremely painful. It is sad to see how many young men and women lack any sense of gratefulness for the sacrifices their parents have made while they were growing up (and often continue to make in order to put them through school or to help establish them on their own). These children are usually the first to turn their backs on the values their parents have tried to instill in them over the years.

When a young adult loses his (or her) moorings entirely or feels that the ground is breaking under his feet, it is best not to argue: rather, simply show by your actions that you

continue to love him. Of course, if he has rejected everything in his upbringing entirely and has no more reverence
whatsoever for God and parents, there is little one can do
other than pray. Often the temptation to coax or persuade a
rebellious child to turn around prevents parents from recognizing this. Some make concessions or threaten all sorts of
reprisals, and others become embittered and disown their
children for good. All of this is useless. The child will only
react by digging in his or her heels. Earnest prayer in the
confidence that God has his hand over every situation and
knows what is best for every person is the only answer.

When the church father Augustine abandoned his faith
as a young man, his mother Monica became desperate with
worry. Finally she went to a mystic and asked him for advice, telling him, "The more I speak to my son about God,
the further he goes astray." The mystic answered her, "Stop
talking to your son about God, and speak to God about
your son." Monica followed his advice, and eventually her
son found his way back to faith.

In certain instances even the most ardent prayers may not
bring the change an anxious parent is looking for. Then all
one can do is to let go of one's child and place his or her
future in God's hands. Kahlil Gibran reminds us:

> Your children are not your children.
> They are the sons and daughters of Life's
> longing for itself...
> You may give them your love but not your thoughts.
> For they have their own thoughts.

You may house their bodies,
but not their souls,
For their souls dwell in the house of tomorrow,
which you cannot visit,
not even in your dreams.[46]

Obviously, we fail in our duty to our children when we let them exercise freedom without helping them to see that it always entails responsibility. The youthful desire for independence is natural enough, but young adults must realize that it cannot exist in a vacuum. We must help them to see that when they cut the apron strings, they tie themselves, whether they like it or not, to new obligations.

One of the best ways to do this – to prepare them simultaneously for the freedoms and responsibilities of adult life – is to give them the firm footing of a further education. Aside from building character, the discipline and concentration developed by a thorough training, whether practical, technical, or academic, will have a direct bearing on their ability to stand on their own feet and earn a living. It will also expose them to conflicting ideas and philosophies of life and help them to test their convictions in settings that require an open mind and a broad heart. (For high school students who are not ready for college or further academic study, volunteer service is often a good option.)

Even if we must guide our children toward adulthood, let us never try to coerce them to follow our path simply because it is the one we have chosen. It is only natural to hope that they will some day find the same security and joy we have in our faith, yet we must refrain from making choices for them. Otherwise they will never find their own way.

Ultimately, we cannot give our children our faith. We can only give them the knowledge that the battle between good and evil – between selflessness and selfishness, light and darkness – must be fought in every heart, and that they, too, must fight it. We can also pass on to them the assurance that if we long to serve God, he will give us the gift of faith. If our children are able to find faith even as small as a mustard seed, they will find strength to face the challenges of life.

CHAPTER THIRTY-THREE

Materialism

A S MENTIONED EARLIER, I spent most of my childhood in the backwoods of South America, and during my first seven years our family lived in acute poverty. For food we sometimes had to be satisfied with the bare minimum: cornmeal mush with molasses. Bread spread with lard and sprinkled with salt was a treat. Yet in spite of the economic hardships, I would find it hard to imagine a happier childhood. Why? Simply because my parents loved us children, and our happiness depended on that – not on toys, treats, or money.

Today, despite the horrendous conditions of many inner-city neighborhoods and the growing threat of financial insecurity to many middle-class homes, most families in our society enjoy unprecedented material standards. Ironically, however, their relative wealth seems to have brought their children little happiness. Often this is because money, work, and the pressures of modern life have pushed children further and further into the background.

Many parents who allow their work to drive them, even at the expense of their children, feel that they have no other choice: they do so in the hope of providing a secure financial future for their children, and for themselves. In itself, this is not to be belittled. Yet if we look at our society (and ourselves, for we make up society) we must admit that all too often what sways our decisions is not really our children, nor even their futures, but money. Certainly it is impossible to live without money and material goods. Every family must earn a living and see to it that money is set aside for the future. In many cases, the demands of work leave few opportunities for regular interaction between parent and child. But ultimately it is the love we give to our children, not the material things, that will remain with them for life. Parents who sacrifice what little time they could spend with their children for better pay would do well to remember this.

An acquaintance recently wrote to me:

> I have seen too many middle-class parents immerse themselves in their work. Working forty to sixty hours a week is a much easier way to get immediate satisfaction. It's much easier to be part of a system with defined rules and objectives and to succeed in a corporate environment. Really taking the time and effort to be an active parent is hard work.

A common excuse for overwork is: "I'm working to put my child through college," or: "We want to pay off our mortgage so that we can leave something for the children." But children don't want an inheritance. They want their parents, now. It's much harder to give yourself and your time to your children now than to work and amass money and in effect buy your children's love.

What does it really mean to give a child love? Many parents, especially those of us who are away from home for days or even weeks at a time, try to deal with our feelings of guilt by bringing home gifts for our children. But we forget that what our children really want, and need, is time and attentiveness, a listening ear and an encouraging word, which are far more valuable than any material thing we can give them.

We cannot deny that, as a whole, our society is driven not by love but by the spirit of materialism, which the Bible calls mammon. Mammon is more than money – it is greed, selfishness, and personal ambition; violence, hatred, and ruthless competition. And it is diametrically opposed to the spirit of childlikeness and of God. In fact, Jesus warns us that if we truly love one, we will despise the other: we cannot serve both.

At times, the spirit of materialism or mammon is openly hostile not only to the childlike spirit, but to children themselves. It is the underlying force behind the whole contraceptive mentality that leads so many people to believe in the "necessity" of population control, both in the sense of "saving" the world from too many children, and in the sense of avoiding individual unwanted pregnancies.

Many people today mistakenly assume that population control will solve many of the problems besetting the globe: crowded cities, unemployment, famine, and pollution. I suspect that the real answer, however, has more to do with learning to accept a lower standard of living, redistributing our wealth, and giving the poorer nations of the world greater access to the resources we squander so freely in the West. As writer Richard John Neuhaus has pointed out, what zero-population-growth advocates fear is "not so much a population explosion as an explosion of population among the poor…in Africa and Asia."[47]

The spirit of mammon is also the root of abortion. The deliberate, legalized killing of the unborn is, I believe, worse than the Massacre of the Innocents in Bethlehem 2000 years ago. No matter how painful or difficult the circumstances of conception or birth, and no matter how debilitated or deformed a baby, we must witness to the fact that every human being is created by God in his image, and that each one has a purpose. To destroy a child, whether born or unborn, is to deface this image of God.

Hundreds of thousands of abortions are performed solely for the sake of personal convenience, or even for the sake of vanity, as recently happened in our neighborhood, when a young woman rejected an offer to take her unwanted child and proceeded with an abortion in order to avoid abdominal stretch marks. It is true that many abortions are also carried out in the name of "love" to a mother who is claimed to be unfit or unable to carry her child to term. Others are argued to be necessary to prevent the emotional turmoil a mother might suffer from bearing a deformed child. Yet even then, we cannot deny that God intends the life in question, even if it only lives for a few hours.

Speaking about abortion, Bonhoeffer says:

> A great many different motives may lead to an action of this kind. Indeed, in cases where it is an act of despair performed in circumstances of extreme human or economic destitution and misery, the guilt may often lie rather with the community than with the individual...These considerations must no doubt have a quite decisive influence on our personal and pastoral attitude towards the person concerned, but they cannot in any way alter the fact of murder.[48]

We can never judge or despise a woman who chooses to abort a child. After all, it is often not her choice alone – in many cases women are pressured into having an abortion by the baby's father or by others. On the other hand we must recognize, as Pope John Paul II has written, that at root every rejection of human life, whatever its form, is really a rejection of Christ.[49]

If we are determined to go the way of Jesus, we must see mammon for what it is – an enemy of childlikeness, of children, and of God. Jesus declared war on the spirit of mammon; his way was and is the way of sharing, of serving and loving others, even if that means bearing a heavy cross.

In fighting the spirit of materialism in ourselves and in our children, let us be reminded that we cannot simply fight "against materialism." Our goal must be something positive – the alternate vision of a life where we seek joy in simple things, find contentment with less rather than more, and encourage each other in generously sharing whatever we have. Child psychologist Robert Coles writes:

> I think that what children in the United States desperately need is a moral purpose, and a lot of our children here aren't getting that. They're getting parents who are very concerned about getting them into the right colleges, buying the best clothes for them, giving them an opportunity to live in neighborhoods where they'll lead fine and affluent lives and where they can be given the best things, to go on interesting vacations, and all sorts of things...Moral vision doesn't only come from what a culture fights against. Moral vision comes from what a people fight for, what they're willing to die for and live for.[50]

In bringing up our children, let us help them to see, as the apostle Paul says, that the material wealth of our world is "uncertain," and teach them to "put their hope in God." Let us "give them a firm foundation for the coming age so that they may take hold of the life that is truly life" (1 Tit. 6:17–18).

CHAPTER THIRTY-FOUR

The Media

FOR MANY PARENTS TODAY, the most frustrating thing
about trying to bring up children according to Christ's
teachings is the constant battle they must wage against the
mass media. In a certain sense this is hardly surprising. After
all, we live in a country where the average child has wit-
nessed an estimated 200,000 televised acts of violence by
the age of sixteen and some 40,000 sexually titillating scenes
by the age of eighteen, not to mention a steady barrage of
programming that glamorizes casual sex, crime, substance
abuse, and occultic practices.[51] There are very few who make
it into adulthood without buying into the values of the
media for at least a short period, and even fewer who come
away without having been desensitized by what they have
seen, heard, and read.

Hour after hour, day after day, our children are bom-
barded by sordid, violent images. And any psychologist will
confirm that these images are not neutral, but press for real-

ization.* Over many years of counseling inmates in county jails and state prisons, I have seen it time after time: our nation's youth are working out their frustrations and their fantasies in the same violent ways that their favorite screen idols do. As writer Mary Pipher has noted, "This is first time in the history of the human race that...kids are learning how to behave from watching TV personae rather than from watching real people."[52]

Even when parents try to swim against the stream, the struggle is often disheartening. At the same time that they are desperately trying to instill the values of responsibility and compassion, modesty and sexual purity in their children, television shows, movies, radio programs, and glossy magazines are doing their best to sell precisely the opposite: irresponsibility, vengefulness, self-centeredness, and promiscuity. In addition, home videos, "adult" phone services, and the Internet (in spite of its incredible positive potentials) are making it easier and easier to bring the wares of porn merchants right into our children's bedrooms.

Unfortunately, things continue to get worse. Despite the warnings of one expert after another, despite the growing number of concerned parents, educators, and pastors – despite even the acknowledgment of the media industry itself that much of what it spews forth is harmful – the offerings of television, radio, and the print media in particular have become increasingly shameless with every passing year.

*See J. Heinrich Arnold, *Freedom from Sinful Thoughts* (Rifton, NY: Plough, 1973), especially the chapters "About Being Beset by Evil" and "Fascination."

Yesterday's pornography has become today's run-of-the-mill advertising.

Perhaps the main reason for our inability to break free from the grip of the media is our lack of initiative in raising our children the way we really want to. Even though many of us are certain that much of what the media exposes them to is devastating for them, we often find it hard to do more than talk about it. This problem is illustrated in a very telling way by an incident involving a colleague of mine who once asked an audience he was speaking to whether they thought television was bad for their children. Every hand in the room shot up. When he asked how many parents were ready to stop their children from watching television, however, not one hand went up.

Part of the problem may also be our unwillingness to admit our own addiction to the media, and to television in particular. Sibyl Sender, a former Madison Avenue editor who is now a member of our Bruderhof, writes:

It seems as if each person says to himself, "But I am different. I have my own values, and nothing I watch or read can affect them. Just because I see a story about killing your grandmother doesn't mean I'm going to rush right out and do it too."

True enough. But each person *has* done things he wishes he hadn't. And the influence of the mass media on your values is very subtle. You don't even know your attitudes are slowly changing.

Let's say you intend to be a good, decent person, trustworthy and friendly and wholesome. If you were offered an all-expense-paid scholarship to the university of murder, arson, and rape, would you accept? If someone invited you to the worship services of a heathen idol would you attend? Of course not.

But the truth is that if you are an average American you have already graduated from the preschool of pornography, the elementary school of horrors, the junior high of junk, and you're working on a Ph.D. in violence unlimited. You have spent more time learning how to live like a criminal than you have in learning anything else your school teaches. That's because during your school years you have spent an average of three hours at the set for every two in the classroom.

Your home has become a temple, your family the congregation, and the TV set the chanting priest of a religion of vileness. You have attended more worship services than a Trappist monk. You thought you were being entertained, but actually you were being preached to.

The tube has been your school and your religion; it may even have been your mother, your father, your sister, and your brother – because you listened to it far more than to any of them. So the tube is your family too.

I don't need to tell you what comes out of the tube. You know. You know its values are not your values in most cases. But you can't stop watching.[53]

Bring up the question of whose fault this is, and you'll hear all sorts of excuses. Many parents feel that what their children watch on television or listen to on the radio is not ultimately their responsibility, but the responsibility of programmers and film makers. Others feel that even if the responsibility is primarily theirs, the government should be doing more to control the excesses. Some worry that to limit their children's exposure to the media will stunt them socially or intellectually and place them at a disadvantage in school. Still others feel it unwise to shield their children from the "hard realities" of the world.

To my mind, these parents are mistaken on several counts. For one thing, the media is a two-way street. Programmers don't broadcast into a vacuum: they give their audiences what they want. Second, the unbelievable moral decay that has taken place in the last decades ought to make it clear that the government is not capable of legislating morality. Third, parents who curtail their children's access to television will find that their children spend more time reading or engaging in other constructive activities. Lastly, it is not merely wise to protect and guide children – it is the only sure way to pass on one's values to them. If we are truly concerned about what our children watch on television, listen to on the radio, or find on the Internet, we will keep a watchful eye on what they are doing. Children accept what they hear and become what they are exposed to.

Pulling the plug on the media, to be sure, is only part of the answer. If television has been our children's primary form of relaxation or entertainment, for instance, we must be as willing to help them find new interests as we are to cut back or eliminate the hours they waste in front of the set. We must also be ready to spend more time with them, and to become involved in their lives in a concrete way.

All the same, two generations of TV-deprived children in our Bruderhof communities, as well as increasing numbers of families across the country (as in Farmington, Connecticut, where the public library initiated a successful "TV-Turn-Off Project") can testify that ridding the home of television is a very good way to begin.[54] Once the set is gone, you'll be surprised to rediscover a whole new world – the real world – around you. More important, you will find that you have never had so much time for your children.

To parents who feel discouraged or lonely in their fight to stand strong against the prevailing currents of our time, let me say this: don't give in, but hold firm. You owe it to God, to yourself, and to your children to educate them in his fear and love.

CHAPTER THIRTY-FIVE

The Breakdown
of the Family

A GAINST THE BACKDROP of all I have written so far about the importance of rearing children in a stable, family-oriented environment stands the harsh reality that it is fast becoming an exception rather than the norm. In a certain sense, it may seem futile to waste breath bemoaning the demise of the family; on the other hand, a discussion of the trend – and a few illustrations of its effect on children – may serve to remind us how often the forces that threaten family life come from within the home itself.

The breakdown of the family is one of the greatest tragedies of our time. It is also one of the most common. Millions of children grow up without even knowing what "family" means – that is, they grow up without the security of a mother and father who love them and love each other.

Tempting as it is, I will not describe the ills of present-day society simply by citing statistics or by presenting another analysis of the problems; plenty of others have done that, and continue to do so, in compelling detail. It is not that the statistics aren't shocking. Every day in America, 22 children are murdered or killed; 1,115 teenage girls have abortions; and 2,860 children see their parents divorce. Every night 100,000 children go to sleep in parks, under bridges, or in homeless shelters.[55] Yet for most of us – and I do not mean to belittle the tremendous suffering these facts and figures represent – they remain mere numbers that startle us momentarily but then quickly lose meaning.

It is the same with analyses of the great social misery around us. The links between the decline of the two-parent family and our society's emphasis on individual self-fulfillment at all costs, for example, are apparent enough. So are the connections between divorce and poverty, child abuse and juvenile delinquency, parental neglect and gang activity, fatherlessness and homosexuality, and underfunded schools and overcrowded detention centers. The list could go on and on.

Many of the problems relating to the breakdown of the family seem to be such a matter of course that they often go unmentioned. Take, for example, the fact that in the United States tax and welfare structures penalize rather than assist people who marry and have children. The result is a rising tide of social horrors that is already dislodging the foundations of our society. What are we doing about it? According to columnist Marilyn Gardner, very little of lasting significance:

Long ago, a popular children's tale tells us, a young boy in Holland discovered a tiny leak in a dike. Knowing his town would be flooded if the dike broke, he stuck his finger in the hole, holding back the ocean until help arrived. The town was spared, and the boy was hailed as a hero.

Today, would-be heroes in this country are using similar finger-in-the-dike approaches as they seek to avert another kind of impending disaster, this one social. Desperate to protect children – and everyone else – from rising floodwaters of violence and aggressive behavior, politicians, executives, teachers, and parents are devising a variety of fingers or plugs to hold danger at bay.

Gardner acknowledges that numerous measures are being taken – commendable, well-meant ones – but, she points out, they often do very little to address the real problems that need to be solved. To prevent children's access to pornography, for instance, some politicians and school administrators recommend the new V-chip; to cut back school yard violence, they propose uniforms; to cure attention-deficit disorders, they advocate the prescription of mind-altering drugs like Ritalin. She concludes:

> In the fictional account of the Dutch boy holding back the sea, men with tools eventually fixed the dike itself. But in real-life America, the answer often appears to involve plugging holes rather than shoring up the social and moral infrastructure. To do that will require a cultural shift – a national willingness to address seriously such issues as the continuing proliferation of violent entertain

ment, the widespread disregard for poor children caught in the crossfire of welfare reform, and the need for more adults willing to take a deep interest in the well-being of young people of all ages and classes.

Desperate hopes need more than frivolous solutions. The cleverest stopgap measures can never be enough when what is called for is a change of priorities and heart.[56]

Hearts and priorities often change slowly, though, and to change them at all will require more than a cultural shift. What we need is a spiritual revolution, one that transforms not only the world "out there" but our own hearts – our own personal lives, our marriages, and the homes we ourselves have created for our children. Perhaps one small way to work for this change is to listen to the voices of those around us whose lives have been torn by violence and pain, and to let their wounds touch us. Below, two friends of mine share how they were affected by divorce and child abuse:

ARI

More than any other event in my life, my parents' divorce...when I was six years old shaped me into the person I am...My earliest memories center on the place where, before the divorce, we briefly called ourselves a family...

Friday night...was a time when, by the magic of the Sabbath candles, we were transformed into a happy, picture-book family. The recriminations and bickering would cease and the music would begin...My mother waved her hands over the lighted candles and covered her eyes as she stood in a silent moment of meditation...

When, a little while later, my father returned from the synagogue, we lined up in front of him for the Sabbath blessing...

On one such Friday night I sensed the perfect opportunity. "I want a dog," I announced between songs.

"Not again," my mother said. "Sweetheart, I already told you, no dogs. Anyway, I think you're allergic to dogs."

"Judy," my father interrupted. "You don't know that for sure, and besides, I don't see the harm – "

"Marvin." Her voice was rising. "Don't contradict me in front of the children." And that was the end of the singing. The music stopped and the candles went out.

Not long after, my parents were divorced. The fight over the dog, of course, had nothing to do with it. It was just another in a series and, no doubt, one of the more benign of their tortured nine-year marriage. But try telling that to a six-year-old boy...

From the perspective of traditional Jewish law, there is nothing wrong with divorce as long as you follow the rabbinic procedures...Such an event is regrettable, but it is certainly doable...Jewish law...makes little provision for those who most suffer the consequences: the children. There is an entire volume of the Talmud that deals with divorce...Still, nowhere in the tractate's 180 pages is there a substantive discussion of the custody of the children. Children get lost in the shuffle of papers and legalisms. Thus, the most serious – and most moral – issue of divorce is sorely ignored.

To my mind, divorce is a deplorable breach of contract, and I say without humor that children should be allowed to sue. Consider the facts: Two people agree to create a human being and promise to give it love, a home, security, and happiness. They take this step with the best of intentions, to be sure, but then something goes awry. They find they really hate each other or for some other reason cannot live together. But in separating, they put themselves first and forget about the contract they have with their child. I do not believe, as you often hear soon-to-be-divorced parents say, that the separation will be "best for the child." My experience has taught me better.

But didn't my parents spare me an unhappy home where fighting and angry confrontation were the mode of communication? I believe not. I believe that they – as incompatible as they were and remain today – could have learned to stop shouting or slamming doors. At least they could have learned all that more easily than I learned to be a child of divorce.

With divorce so common these days, mine is not a popular position. Some – usually divorced people with children – accuse me of being selfish. But it's not just me. Someday they will hear it from their own children. A lost childhood cannot be recaptured.[57]

CHARLENE

When I was in kindergarten our class often took walks. If our parents had given us spending change, we were allowed to buy candy from a store we passed. My parents always forgot these days.

One morning my sister and I walked into my parents' bedroom and found my mother's purse open. Instead of asking for money, my sister took a bill out of Mom's wallet. When my parents awoke, my mother noticed (she was planning to shop for groceries that day) that a $100 bill she had put in her wallet was gone. My father started to yell at her, and my parents searched the house high and low for the money. In the meantime, my sister handed me the money to hold.

Soon, my Mom started to cry. I knew the money was the cause for it, so I handed her the money and asked her to stop crying. My Dad, witnessing this, flew into a rage: "What did I tell you I would do if I caught you stealing?" The answer was that he would burn our hands off.

I pleaded and pleaded with him, and told him that I had not stolen the money, but when he asked me how then I had gotten it, I didn't want to get my sister into trouble. My Dad turned on the stove until it was cherry red and made me place my hand on the burner.

I begged and begged him not to make me, and looked to my mother to try to gain sympathy, to try to get her to talk Dad out of it, but nothing worked. My father said, "I am only doing this because I love you." Then he placed my hand on the burner. I guess I passed out, because I don't remember anything after that except waking up in a children's hospital with my hand bandaged. The burns had gone all the way to the bone.

From then on, every time my father hit me he would

always justify it by saying, "I'm only doing this because I love you." It wasn't until I was fourteen years old that I realized that other children were not "loved" by their fathers in the same way.

In the locker room at high school, a classmate once questioned the bruises and welts I had. I tried to explain that it was my fault – I had provoked my father. She told me that it was not my wrong, but my father's in not being able to control his temper. I ended the conversation quickly – I did not want to hear negative things about my Dad.

One night my father came home after a hard day and once again flew into a rage. This was typical: whenever we heard our father's car pulling into the garage, we became nervous, because we feared his moods. Needless to say, he beat me so terribly that I needed to be hospitalized. By some strange coincidence, the doctor who attended to me was the same doctor who had attended to me about ten years earlier, the burned-hand incident. Seeing me once again and remembering our last encounter, he threatened my mother. She had no choice but to ask my father to leave and get help. My father did not feel he needed help, and inevitably my parents were divorced. My mother, who still loved my father, blamed me for the divorce…After years of resentment we're finally starting to become friends.[58]

Ari and Charlene are only two out of many millions of people who have suffered at the hands of their parents. Yet to me their experiences stand out in a special way, even if they might be matched or superseded by other, perhaps far-worse stories. Maybe that is because I know the faces and voices behind them – faces that do not permit me to analyze or explain, but only to respond with my heart. For anyone concerned about the breakdown of the family, perhaps this is the most important challenge: to seek those around us who suffer its effects, and to reach out to them – not in pity, but with love.

CHAPTER THIRTY-SIX

The Need
for Community

I F THERE IS ANYTHING I would like to leave the reader at
the close of this book, it is Foerster's simple reminder that
with respect to education in particular, it is never the mere
word, but the word become flesh, that frees. It is one thing
to read (or write) a book about educating children, but
quite another to actually do it. Words, after all, are easy to
come by, and so are theories and ideas, anecdotes and suggestions. For that matter, so are PTA meetings, conferences,
and forums. Workable solutions are much harder to find.
Yet without them, without positive, practical outcomes, all
of the many good things we do in the name of education are
useless. In the end, each of us – parents, grandparents, aunts
or uncles, teachers, mentors, or friends – must find concrete
ways to meet the individual needs of the children entrusted
to our care and guide them toward adulthood.

To raise children is certainly a privilege and a joy, but it is
also a great responsibility that demands prayer, patience,

and hard work. These days it often seems a daunting task and requires courage as never before. According to an ancient saying that has become one of the most repeated educational slogans of our decade, it takes a whole village to raise a child. The thought is definitely a valid one: parents represent only two of the many factors influencing a child's development. The messages he receives from teachers, from those around him, and from society at large have every bit as much bearing on him as those he receives at home. For any of them to be effective or successful, they must work together. As William Damon, a noted author and professor of education, puts it, a parent may "offer a sterling example for the child," a teacher may provide the complement of insights and admonition, but in the long run a child will experience confusion unless he or she finds "synchronous notes elsewhere in the community."[59]

There is very little harmony in our society today. Parents, educators, experts, and policy-makers often contradict and sometimes even undermine each other. In fact, it seems that the wider "community" is more of an unattainable ideal than a reality, and that in many (if not most) cases, the proverbial village simply does not exist. Dostoyevsky, never one to shy from calling a spade a spade, named the root cause for this already more than a century ago:

> Everyone strives to keep his individuality as apart as possible, wishes to secure the greatest possible fullness of life for himself; but meantime all his efforts result not in attaining fullness of life but self-destruction, for instead of

self-realization he ends by arriving at complete solitude. All mankind in our age have split up into units, they all keep apart, each in his own groove; each one holds aloof, hides himself and hides what he has from the rest, and he ends by being repelled by others and repelling them...He sinks into self-destructive impotence, for he is accustomed to rely upon himself alone and to cut himself off from the whole; he has trained himself not to believe in the help of others, in men and in humanity...[60]

In a sense, Dostoyevsky's indictment might seem pessimistic or depressing. Yet it can also be taken as a challenge – an acknowledgment of our present situation and, as such, an important first step toward change. Even if we are still imprisoned in our egos, we must believe that we can be freed, and that we can build communities for our children, communities where parents and educators, grown-ups and children, strive to meet the same goals.

Utopian as it might sound to some, I am convinced that this is possible wherever men and women are ready to sacrifice self-interest for a greater common good. A few cases in point are the highly regarded schools of the Hutterites in 16th- and 17th-century Europe, where children, parents, and teachers lived and worked together in the manner of the early Christians; the ashrams of India, where, as Tagore once wrote, "the young and the old, the teacher and the student, sit at the same table to take their daily food and the food of eternal life"; the schools of our present-day Bruderhof communities; and the small but growing number of public schools where parents, teachers, and administrators are showing that it is possible not only to interact but to work together and achieve positive results.[61]

Admittedly, healthy educational communities have always been few and far between. Progress is hardly ever dramatic; in fact, it is usually very slow. As every parent and teacher knows, education is never a matter of ten-step plans or quick formulas, but of faithful commitment to the mundane challenges of daily life: getting up from the sofa to spend time with our children, loving them and disciplining them, becoming involved in their lives at school and, most important, making sure they have a wholesome family life to return to at home. Maybe that is why Jesus teaches us to ask for strength little by little, on a daily basis – "Give us this day our daily bread" – and why he stresses the significance of even the smallest, humblest beginnings: "Wherever two of you agree about anything you ask for, it shall be done for you...For where two or three come together in my name, I shall be with them" (Mt. 18:19–20).

Almost three thousand years have passed since Isaiah wrote of a peaceable kingdom, an eternal community where "the wolf shall dwell with the lamb...and a little child shall lead them" (Isa. 11:6). No matter how dark or foreboding the chaos of our present world, let us never forget the prophet's wonderful vision and the greatness of God that stands behind it. Far off as it seems, we can and must help each other to press on toward it – brother by brother, sister by sister, child by child.

Endnotes

1. Paraphrased from Eberhard Arnold, *"Der Kampf um die Kindheit" (1928), Archives of the Bruderhof Communities, EA 28/5.*

2. From *"Nachschriften"* (January 8, 1911), an unpublished collection of sermons in the Archives of the Bruderhof Communities.

3. Bruderhof Communities, eds., *Community Alive Today*, No. 14 (December 1995), 1.

4. Christopher Zimmerman, "A Conversation with Jonathan Kozol," *Plough* 47 (Spring 1996), 11.

5. Maggie Gallagher, *The Abolition of Marriage,* quoted in John Leo, "Where Marriage Is a Scary Word." *US News & World Report* (February 5, 1996), 22.

6. Dietrich Bonhoeffer, *Letters and Papers from Prison* (New York: Macmillan, 1973), 42–46.

7. For further discussion of the themes in this chapter, see my book *A Plea for Purity: Sex, Marriage, and God* (Plough, 1996).

8. Joseph Lucas, *Mutter, forme uns,* n.d., n.p.

9. Philip Britts, "Presentation of Margaret Ann Wright," Loma Hoby, December 5, 1948 (Archives of the Bruderhof Communities S–257).

10. Dorothy Day, *Meditations,* selected by Stanley Vishnewski (New York: Newman Press, 1970), 10.

11. Mumia Abu-Jamal, "Mother-loss," *Plough* 44 (July–August 1995), 10.

12. Ralph Kinney Bennett, "What Kids Need Most in a Dad, " *Reader's Digest* (February 1992), 94.

13. Michael E. Phillips, *To Be a Father Like the Father* (Camp Hill, PA: Christian Publications, 1992), 24.

14. Teresa de Bertodano, comp. *Daily Readings with Mother Teresa* (London: HarperCollins, 1993), 136.

15. Friedrich Froebel, *The Education of Man* (New York: D. Appleton, 1900; reprinted by Augustus M. Kelley, Clifton, NJ, 1974), 55–56.

16. Society of Brothers, eds., *Children in Community* (Rifton, NY: Plough, 1975), 62.

17. Rod Moscr, "Those Wee Hours of the Night: Nocturnal Enuresis in Children," *Advance* (May 1994), 13–15.

18. Clyde Haberman, "Their Loss of Respect Starts at Home." *New York Times* (February 20, 1996).

19. J. Heinrich Arnold, *Discipleship*, (Farmington, PA: Plough, 1994; 4th printing 1996) 169.

20. J. Christoph Blumhardt and Christoph F. Blumhardt, *Thoughts About Children* (Rifton, NY: Plough, 1980), 28–29.

21. Eberhard Arnold, *The Early Christians After the Death of the Apostles* (Rifton, NY: Plough, 1970), 178.

22. J. H. Arnold, *Discipleship*, 196.

23. John Paul II, *Evangelium Vitae*. English ed., *Origins* 24:42 (April 6, 1995), 694–695.

24. Jean Vanier, *Community and Growth*, 2nd revised ed. (New York: Paulist, 1989), 96.

25. J.C. and C.F. Blumhardt, 14–15.

26. E. Arnold, *Education*, 7 8.

27. Froebel, 124.

28. F.W. Foerster, *Hauptaufgaben der Erziehung* (Freiburg: Herder Verlag, 1959), 70.

29. Hutterian Brethren, eds., *Chronicle of the Hutterian Brethren*, Vol.I (Rifton, NY: Plough, 1987), 64.

30. Edmondo de Amicis, *The Heart of a Boy*, trsl. Sophie Jewett (New York: Frederick Ungar, 1960), 203–207.

31. Fyodor Dostoyevsky, *The Brothers Karamazov*, trsl. Constance Garnett (New York: Random House, The Modern Library, 1950), 383.

32. J.C. and C.F. Blumhardt, 6.

33. Froebel, 55.

34. Henry D. Thoreau, *On Man and Nature*. Compil. Arthur G. Volkman (Mount Vernon, NY: Peter Pauper Press, 1960), 23.

35. Zimmerman, 13.

36. Sheryl WuDunn, "In Japan, Even Toddlers Feel the Pressure to Excel," *The New York Times* (January 23, 1996).

37. William Provine, quoted in Phillip E. Johnson, *Darwin on Trial*, 2nd ed. (Downers Grove, IL: InterVarsity Press, 1993), 126–127.

38. E. Arnold, *Education*, 14.

39. Kenneth Prager, M.D. "Abstinence is Best," *Cortlandt Forum* (January 1994), 140.

40. Shinichi Suzuki, *Nurtured by Love: A New Approach to Education* (Smithtown, N.Y.: Exposition Press, 1969), 95.

41. Quoted in "Points to Ponder," *Reader's Digest* (May 1991), 31.

42. "Champion of Children," *Plough* 12 (September/October 1985), 8.

43. Rachel Carson, *The Sense of Wonder* (New York: Harper & Row, 1965), 88–89.

44. Home School Legal Defense, PO Box 159, Palonian Springs, VA 22129.

45. J.C. and C.F. Blumhardt, 23.

46. Kahlil Gibran, *The Prophet* (New York: Alfred A. Knopf, 1957), 18.

47. Quoted in John Burger, "Greatest Resource: Father Neuhaus discusses population explosion fears," *Catholic New York* (March 14, 1996), 34.

48. Joan Winmill Brown, ed., *The Martyred Christian: 160 Readings by Dietrich Bonhoeffer* (New York: Macmillan, 1983), 114.

49. John Paul II, *Evangelium vitae,* conclusion, no. 102.

50. Quoted in William Bausch, *Becoming A Man* (Mystic, CT: Twenty-Third Publications, 1988), 194–195.

51. Thomas Lickona, *Educating for Character: How Our Schools Can Teach Respect and Responsibility* (New York: Bantam, 1992), 5.

52. Quoted in Deirdre Donahue, "No-Nonsense Therapist Takes Society to Task," *USA Today* (April 9, 1996), D1–2.

53. Hutterian Brethren, eds., *A Straight Word to Kids and Parents* (Rifton, NY: Plough, 1987), 6–7.

54. Lickona, 408.

55. Children's Defense Fund statistics in *Salt of the Earth* (November/December 1995), 13.

56. Marilyn Gardner, "When Fingers in the Dike Can't Stop a Flood," *Christian Science Monitor* (March 7, 1996), 13.

57. Ari L. Goldman, *The Search for God at Harvard* (New York: Random House, 1991), 53–58.

58. From a letter to the author, March 13, 1996.

59. William Damon, *Greater Expectations* (New York: The Free Press, 1995), 242.

60. Dostoyevsky, 363.

61. Amiya Chakravarty, *A Tagore Reader* (New York: Macmillan, 1961), 279.

About the Author

J. Christoph Arnold has served as senior elder of the Bruderhof (approx. 2500 members in eight communities in the US and England) since 1983. He has traveled the world extensively on behalf of the movement and met with religious leaders of many faiths, including Pope John Paul II. Earlier, from 1972 to 1982, he served as a minister and assistant elder of the Bruderhof communities.

Christoph and his wife, Verena, have eight children and fourteen grandchildren. In addition to counseling hundreds of couples, single men and women, teenagers, and prison inmates over many years, they have also provided pastoral care for the terminally ill and their families.

In the last twelve months Christoph has authored three books: *A Plea for Purity: Sex, Marriage, and God; A Little Child Shall Lead Them: Hopeful Parenting in a Confused World;* and *I Tell You a Mystery: Life, Death, and Eternity.* He is currently working on a fourth, *Seventy Times Seven,* on the importance of forgiveness in daily living. Grounded in the experience of the Bruderhof, a community movement based on Christ's teachings and the practices of the earliest believers, these titles are more than books: they bring to expression the life and faith of a whole church.

Christoph is managing editor of *The Plough,* the Bruderhof's quarterly journal. An active speaker, he has appeared as a guest on numerous television and radio programs, and on seminary and college campuses.

About the Bruderhof

BASIS

DESPITE ALL THAT TROUBLES OUR SOCIETY, we must witness to the fact that God's spirit is at work in the world today. God still calls men and women away from the systems of injustice to his justice, and away from the old ways of violence, fear, and isolation to a new way of peace, love, and brotherhood. In short, he calls us to community.

The basis of our communal life is Christ's Sermon on the Mount and his other New Testament teachings, in particular those concerning brotherly love and love of enemies, mutual service, nonviolence and the refusal to bear arms, sexual purity, and faithfulness in marriage. Instead of holding assets or property privately, we share everything in common, the way the early Christians did as recorded in the Book of Acts. Each member gives his or her talents, time, and efforts wherever they are needed. Money and possessions are pooled voluntarily, and in turn each member is provided for and cared for. Lunch and dinner are eaten together, and meetings for fellowship, singing, prayer, or decision making are held several evenings a week.

VISION

Though we come from many cultures, countries, and walks of life, we are all brothers and sisters. We are conscious of our shortcomings as individuals and as a community, yet we believe that it is possible to live out in deeds Jesus' clear way of love, freedom, and truth – not only on Sundays, but from day to day. With Eberhard Arnold we affirm:

> This planet, the earth, must be conquered for a new kingdom, a new social order, a new unity, a new joy. Joy comes to us from God, who is the God of love, who is the spirit of peace, unity, and community. This is the message Jesus brings. And we must have the faith and the certainty that his message is valid still today.

FAMILY LIFE & EDUCATION

Although many of our members are single adults, the family is the primary unit of our community. Children are a central part of our life together. Parents are primarily responsible for educating them, but teachers, as all adult members of our communities, support them with encouragement and, where necessary, guidance. In this way, problems can be solved, burdens carried, and joys shared.

While parents are at work, babies and small children receive daily care in our "Children's House," where the daily schedule reflects the strong influence of the German educational reformers Froebel and Pestalozzi; they felt, as we do, that children need a place where they can truly be children.

Preschool, kindergarten, and elementary grades are educated in our own schools. Although the schedule is geared to a certain extent to integrating the children in the public school system after 8th grade, the classrroom curriculum is run in tandem with a daily program of non-academic activities: arts and crafts, music, sports, nature study, hiking, field trips, and work projects. From the 9th grade, teens attend public high school and then move on to university, college, or technical/vocational training. Some young adults find work in mission service projects and return with valuable knowledge and experience.

Our disabled, invalid, and elderly members are a treasured part of the community. Whether participating in the communal work (even if only for a few hours a day) or remaining at home, where they are often visited by children, they enrich our life in a vital way.

WORK

Our life is a joyful one, as full of the sounds of song and play as of work. We earn our living by manufacturing and selling Community Playthings (a line of play equipment and furniture for children) and Rifton Equipment for People with Disabilities. Other enterprises include a charter flight service and breeding kennels. To us, work is far more than a business venture, however. From washing clothes and dishes to assembling products in our workshops or caring for children, it is a practical expression of our love for one another.

ROOTS

The roots of the Bruderhof go back to the time of the Radical Reformation of early 16th-century Europe, when thousands of so-called Anabaptists left the institutional church to seek a life of simplicity, brotherhood, and nonviolence.

One branch of this dissident movement, known as Hutterites after their leader Jakob Hutter, settled in communal villages or Bruderhofs ("place of brothers") in Moravia. Here their excellent craftsmanship, their advanced medical skills, their agricultural successes, and, most of all, their progressive schools – which attracted even the children of noblemen – brought them widespread renown.

Recent History

In 1920, Eberhard Arnold, a well-known lecturer and writer, left the security of his Berlin career and moved with his wife and children to Sannerz, a tiny German village, to found a small community based on the practices of the early church. Though the Arnolds were not directly influenced by the early Hutterites in founding their new settlement, they soon discovered that Hutterian Bruderhofs still existed (now in North America), and they initiated a relationship that lasts to this day.

Despite persecution by the Nazis and the turmoil of World War II, the community survived. Amid increasing difficulties in Germany (and expulsion in 1937), new Bruderhofs were founded in England in the late 1930s. With the outbreak of World War II a second migration was necessary, this time to Paraguay, the only country willing to accept our multinational group. During the 1950s branch communities were started in the United States and Europe. In 1960–61 the South American communities were closed, and members relocated to Europe and the United States.

THE PRESENT

Today there are three Bruderhofs in New York, one in Connecticut, two in Pennsylvania, and two in southeastern England. We are insignificant in numbers, yet we believe our task is of utmost importance: to follow Jesus and, in a society that has turned against him, to build up a new society guided by his spirit of love. Our movement struggles forward against the stream of contemporary society – and against the obstacles our human weaknesses continually place in the way – yet God has held us together through times of external persecution, internal struggle, and spiritual decline, and we entrust our future to him.

OUTREACH

At a local level, we are involved in voluntary community service projects and prison ministry. On a broader scale, our contacts with other fellowships and community groups have taken us to many places around the globe, especially in recent years. Mission has always been a vital focus of our activity, though not in the sense of trying to convert people or to recruit new members. The connections we make with others outside our communities – with all men and women who strive for brotherhood, no matter what their creed – are just as important to us. Naturally we welcome every person who is seeking something new in his or her life. Come join us for a weekend.

THE PLOUGH PUBLISHING HOUSE

Our publishing house, which is owned and run by Bruderhof members, sells books about radical Christian discipleship, community, marriage, child rearing, social justice, and the spiritual life. We also publish a small periodical, *The Plough,* with articles on current issues the mainstream media tends to ignore, and reflective pieces on personal and societal transformation. Sample copies are available free on request, though we welcome donations to meet costs.

INFORMATION

For more information, or to arrange a visit, write or call The Plough at either of the following addresses. We can give you the address and telephone number of the Bruderhof nearest you :

The Plough Publishing House
Spring Valley Bruderhof, Route 381 N
Farmington PA 15437-9506
Tel: 800/521-8011 or 412/329-1100

or

Darvell Bruderhof
Robertsbridge, E. Sussex
TN32 5DR ENGLAND
Tel: 0800-269-048 or +44 (0) 1580-881-003

www.bruderhof.org

The author with Pope John Paul II, New York City, October 1995

"Before leaving on a vacation I would like quickly to send you a word of warm thanks for the galley proof of your new book about raising children. The moral and educational statements it contains agree completely with what the Holy Father is tirelessly teaching. I am happy that the book is written in a way that is easy to grasp and indeed very beautiful, so that even simple people are able to understand it."

From a letter, Joseph Cardinal Ratzinger
to Johann Christoph Arnold, July 24, 1996

Other Titles from Plough

A PLEA FOR PURITY: SEX, MARRIAGE, AND GOD by Johann Christoph Arnold. Thoughts on relationships, sex, marriage, divorce, abortion, homosexuality, and other related issues from a biblical perspective.

I TELL YOU A MYSTERY: LIFE, DEATH, AND ETERNITY by Johann Christoph Arnold. Drawing on stories of people he has counseled over many years, Arnold addresses the universal human fear of ageing and purposelessness, and shows that even today, in our culture of isolation and death, there is such a thing as hope.

GOD'S REVOLUTION by Eberhard Arnold. Topically arranged excerpts from the author's talks and writings on the church, community, marriage and family issues, government, and world suffering.

THE GOSPEL IN DOSTOYEVSKY An introduction to the "great God-haunted Russian" comprised of passages from *The Brothers Karamazov*, *Crime and Punishment*, and *The Idiot*.

SALT AND LIGHT by Eberhard Arnold. Talks and writings on the transformative power of a life lived by Jesus' revolutionary teachings in the Sermon on the Mount.

248.845
A756

97219

LINCOLN CHRISTIAN COLLEGE AND SEMINARY

DISCIPLESHIP: LIVING FOR CHRIST IN THE DAILY GRIND by J. Heinrich Arnold. A collection of thoughts on following Christ in the daily grind, topically arranged. Includes sections on love, humility, forgiveness, leadership, gifts, community, sexuality, marriage, parenting, illness, suffering, mission, salvation, and the kingdom of God.

THE EARLY CHRISTIANS by Eberhard Arnold. Letters and sayings of the early church in the words of its own members. Includes material from a variety of contemporary sources.

WHY WE LIVE IN COMMUNITY by Eberhard Arnold, with two interpretive talks by Thomas Merton. Inspirational thoughts on the basis, meaning, and purpose of community.

LOVE AND MARRIAGE IN THE SPIRIT by Eberhard Arnold. Talks and essays on the importance of faith as a basis for meaningful and lasting Christian relationships.

INNER LAND: A GUIDE TO THE HEART AND SOUL OF THE BIBLE by Eberhard Arnold. Timeless essays on the "inner land of the invisible" where men and women may find strength and courage to follow God's call in today's world.

TO ORDER
(U.S.): 1-800-521-8011 OR 412-329-1100
(U.K.): 0800-269-048 OR +44(0)1580-881-003
WWW.BRUDERHOF.ORG

3 4711 00149 7959